Escape the Bakasura Trap

Escape the Bakasura Trap

Let Contentment Fuel Your Growth

Devdutt Pattanaik

Illustrations by the author

JUGGERNAUT BOOKS
C-I-128, First Floor, Sangam Vihar, Near Holi Chowk,
New Delhi 110080, India

First published by Juggernaut Books 2025

Copyright © Devdutt Pattanaik 2025

10 9 8 7 6 5 4 3 2 1

P-ISBN: 9789353453749
E-ISBN: 9789353456283

All rights reserved. No part of this publication may be reproduced, transmitted, or stored in a retrieval system in any form or by any means without the written permission of the publisher.

Typeset in Adobe Caslon Pro by Dhaivat Chhaya, Mumbai

Printed at Replika Press Pvt. Ltd, India

To Shamsi, and the cream roll

'Approach this book with curiosity, not combat.'

Contents

A Trap and an Escape	1
Step 1 of 3: Eat Better, to Nourish Your 'Business' Body	35
Step 2 of 3: Kill Less, to Retrain Your 'Behavioural' Body	79
Step 3 of 3: Feed More, to Sensitize Your 'Belief' Body	123
Bhima's Contentment	173
Workbooks	185

A Trap and an Escape

Bakasura is a character in the 2,000-year-old Hindu epic Mahabharata. He was so hungry that he ate even those who fed him. This made him infamous as the demon of hunger.

Hunger is translated as 'bhaksha' in Sanskrit and 'baka' in Prakrit. Asura means a demon, one who takes, who opposes Deva, a god, one who gives. Bhaksha-asura, that is, Bakasura, has been made the role model of modern consumer society. Here, we are told to be hungry all the time. Capitalists are hungry for profit; socialists are hungry for justice; libertarians are hungry for freedom. The more we consume, the more we grow. The biggest are ravenous all the time.

Success in modern consumer society is about having more than others. Children are being told by parents, teachers, entertainers, journalists and leaders that they will be valued if they have more: more resources, more pleasure, more leisure, more money, more power, more status, more fame, more glamour, more information, more influence, more fans, more followers, more productivity, more wins, more likes.

No one talks about the cost of consumption. The production of anything consumed involves violence. By asking children to have more, we are asking children to kill more. The educated today do not use this language. Ancient Indian sages did.

Known as Rishis, the ones who see what others do not see, these ancient Indian sages said: Hunger (bhaksha) leads to consumption (bhoga), which demands sacrifice (bali), which has consequences (karma) that trap us in the wheel of rebirth (samsara). Eating creates debt (paap). Feeding creates credit (punya). When there is no debit or credit, there is freedom (moksha). This was known to Jain, Buddhist and Hindu merchants, hence the accounting vocabulary. But we have forgotten these ideas. We are now under the spell of Western 'enlightenment'.

Modern vocabulary is filled with words of judgement: right and wrong, good and bad, justified, ethical and moral. It is always the winner who decides who is right and what is wrong. So powerful is this spell that Indians, since the nineteenth century, have translated the word 'dharma' as 'righteousness'. This ignores the accounting paradigm. We have forgotten what dharma used to mean: acts that reduce debt. To reduce debt, we have to stop eating and start feeding. But how can we feed others if we are possessed by

A Trap and an Escape

the demon of hunger? Instructions will not help. Wisdom is needed. Awareness of other people's truth. Sensitivity to other people's hunger. The sage can only give knowledge. Wisdom is an individual's journey. That is why in Hindu mythology, there are no prophets or messengers. Just yogis and avatars, such as Hara (Shiva) and Hari (Vishnu), who nudge both the Asuras and the Devas. The world of Indian myth has no sense of urgency: There is no end of the world, no climax. There is endless eternity (sanatan). We change for our sake, not for the sake of the world. We change because wisdom brings bliss, contentment, kindness and an ecosystem of abundance around us.

Nature	Hermit's World	Householder Culture
Hunger (Bhaksha)	Hunger (Bhaksha)	Hunger (Bhaksha)
↓	↓	↓
Violence (Himsa)	Non-Violence (Ahimsa)	Violence (Himsa)
↓	↓	↓
Eating (Bhoga)	Fasting (Yoga)	Feeding (Naivedya)
↓	↓	↓
Debt (Paap-karma)	No Debt (Shunya)	Credit (Punya-karma)
↓	↓	↓
Being Eaten (Samsara)	Freedom (Moksha)	Being Fed (Prasad)

Escape the Bakasura Trap

Today, hunger is marketed as aspiration and ambition. It is being fuelled with comparison and competition. Everything is being tracked: targets to achieve, tasks to complete. The poor are being motivated to become rich; the rich are being inspired to become richer; the richest are being frightened so that they never leave the killing fields. They must be the biggest canine in the dog-eat-dog world, the fastest rodent in the rat race, the scariest fish in the shark tank. Endless conflict is thus being manufactured between those who consume and those who get consumed, those with surplus and those without access.

We genuinely believe that consuming food and hoarding food will take away hunger. But it only creates addicts. Winners feel successful, but soon, a new target is in sight, a new game, a new goalpost. Losers are resentful, seeking justice: more rights, more opportunities, more reservations, more subsidies, more freedom, more equality, more fairness. Even revolutions have been gamified. Everyone feels tricked, cheated, cancelled, deprived, denied, exiled, victimized. Everyone is locked in a war room, strategizing to crush the competition and emerge triumphant. But the siege of the losers never ends. This ecosystem of inequality, anxiety, pollution and violence is the Bakasura Trap.

A Trap and an Escape

Belief of Capitalists and Socialists	Belief of Rishis	Householder Culture
Hunger + Food ↓ Satisfaction	Hunger + Food ↓ Addiction ↓ Extraction, Hoarding, Raiding, Trickery	Hunger + Food + Empathy (other people's truth) ↓ Contentment ↓ Exchange

To escape, we first need to appreciate:
- How overestimating science and technology has shifted our focus from hunger to food
- How reclaiming myth brings our focus back to hunger, especially the hunger for meaning, which remains, technological shifts notwithstanding
- How modern values are essentially Western, not global, or rational
- How modern notions of success are actually mythical, amplified with the arrogance of technology
- How the Indian epic Mahabharata, seen as the book of war and victory, is actually a meditation on contentment

Only then will Hanuman's intervention in the epic Mahabharata make sense. And it will help us construct the three-step Bhima escape.

Overestimating Science

Animals do not have science, or stories. Humans have both. Because humans can imagine. We can conjure up possibilities outside the realm of experience. We can imagine food coming to us, feeling warm in snow, flying beyond the horizon and swimming under the stars. We can imagine being in control of everything around us: the river, the wind, the plants, the animals, even fellow humans. This compels us to make sense of the world, find causes, consequences and connections between objects and organisms. We observe, we infer, we compare, we find explanations that we can exploit to make life better. This methodical way of thinking is logic, from the Greek word 'logos' for analysis. The Sanskrit word for logic is 'shastra'.

War-zone Imagination	Nature's Reality
Dog-eat-dog world	Eater gets eaten
Rat-race	Killer gets killed
Shark-tank	Parasites kill themselves
War-room	No dominant species
Leaders and Followers	Every organism is predator and prey, and has predator and prey
Winners and Losers	
Stories of heroes and martyrs	Alpha replaced by meritocracy.
Eat but do not get eaten	Queen bee exists for next hive not other way round.
	Pack feeds the young
	Herd protects the young

A Trap and an Escape

The application of logic to life is rationality. Humans have used rational ways of thinking, involving trial and error and the study of patterns, to create technology. Technology has existed long before science. Every tribe had its own technology which helped desert tribes weather sandstorms, and coastal tribes discover new islands. Technology was jealously guarded by tribes. It was accepted from elders on faith, as it had enabled earlier generations to survive. It was transmitted and refined over generations.

Along with technology came stories that also helped tribal elders explain to the terrified and confused next-generation the origin of the world, the purpose of life, and the nature of the afterlife. Stories explained borders, hierarchies, taboos, establishing beliefs and customs about who to include, who to not include, who to serve, who to exploit, who to trust, who to fear. Inherited knowledge ensured survival. These were the cultural truths of the community, referred to as myths, from the Greek word 'mythos' or narrative. The Sanskrit word for myth is 'akhyana'.

A myth is a belief system: true to the insider, false to the outsider. Unlike a folktale, myth is not meant to entertain. Unlike a parable or fable, myth has no prescription. A myth is not propaganda to cover up a lie or to rouse the rabble. A myth exists to provide meaning: provide a community with a common lens to engage with the world. Logos and mythos constituted the knowledge system of a tribe. Logos transmitted technology. Mythos provided meaning.

Different knowledge systems existed in each and every tribe of the pre-modern world, until the rise of science in Europe.

Science rose at a time when Europeans were doubting their dominant myth – that the Christian God and His Church were all-powerful and all-knowing. This followed the defeat of Christians by Muslims during the Crusades, about a thousand years ago. Disillusioned Christians began relooking at pre-Christian mythos and logos, especially those of the Greeks. Simultaneously, thanks to trade with Arabs, Europeans were exposed to new ideas like mathematics from India and new technology like paper, gunpowder and the magnetic compass from China. This fuelled an age of curiosity which eventually led to the birth of science. Later, Europeans would credit the Greeks for this transformation, ignoring the contribution of the Arabs, Indians and Chinese.

Science rejected testimony as the source of knowledge. It was sceptical of inherited knowledge from religion or tradition. It rejected subjectivity. To be real, an observation had to be measurable and verifiable. Microscopes and telescopes revealed worlds that the eye could not see. Experiments showed possibilities that had never been transmitted by any holy book or sage. Human opinion took second place to evidence. Argument was left to philosophers. Scientists sought proof.

Technology and engineering born out of science were far more logical than pre-modern inherited technology – far

A Trap and an Escape

more efficient, far more effective, far more productive. This new technology was universal, not rooted in culture. It improved the capacity and capability of the Europeans enormously, enabling them to discover new sea routes, win wars, establish colonies, build empires, extract resources, develop industries and create ways of living that allowed them to dominate the world. The rise of the engineering world was enabled by the rise of the financial world, with new ways of accounting, banking and raising funds through stock markets. The modern age was thus inaugurated by the industrialized imperial powers of the eighteenth century. Every culture around the world would eventually submit to this new Western way.

The West challenged everything and everyone that existed before and elsewhere. It saw faith as the problem, the source of oppression and violence. It pushed for the erasure of tradition, religion, myths, tribes, clans, castes, monarchies. The old ways had to be replaced by more scientific ways, where inputs and outputs could be measured and modified with feedback. Old hierarchies based on race, gender and sexuality were torn down and replaced by secular nation states that valued liberty, equality and justice for all.

- Capitalism was the logical way to generate wealth.
- Socialism was the logical way to distribute wealth.
- Democracy was the right way to distribute power.
- Universities were the right way to distribute and improve on knowledge.

- Feminism challenged traditional gender roles and refused to accept heterosexuality as the norm.

But while science helped created vast wealth in the nineteenth century, it failed to distribute wealth fairly between nations and within nations. In the late twentieth century, social sciences revealed the unequal distribution of wealth and power. These were being rationalized and justified based on laws but made little moral and ethical sense. It became increasingly evident that while measurements were objective, values were not.

Values were shaped by community, creed, caste, class, race, gender and sexuality. Logic, with measurement and evidence, was being used to create better science and technology for all. Logic, without measurement and evidence, was being used to come up with clever arguments to serve the interests of a few. As a result, despite technological progress, the modern world of the 'civilized' was as violent and as unequal as the pre-modern world of the 'savages'. Worse, it was terribly polluted.

The wrath of postmodern philosophers in the twenty-first century gave rise to the woke movement, which cancelled modern arguments, rejected all structures and sought radical social justice for all, a world free of hierarchies and borders. The woke movement even weaponized fragility, by declaring all challenges to itself offensive and hurtful.

A Trap and an Escape

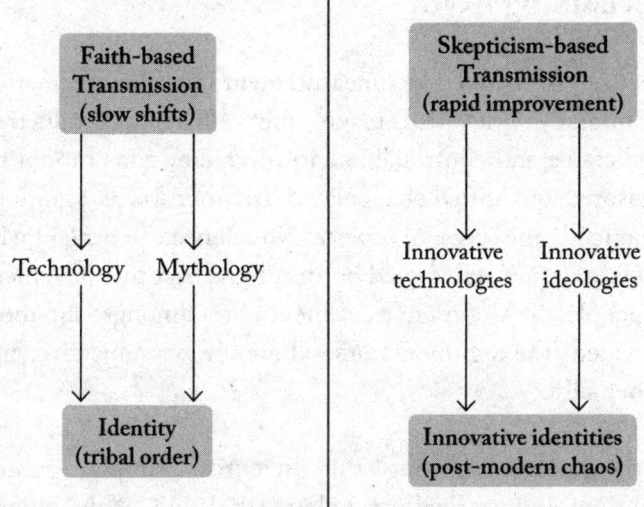

Meanwhile, pre-modern religions and traditions have begun resurrecting themselves with a vengeance, pointing to the failure of science to keep its promises. The problem was never with technology. Science addressed the problem of food. It ignored the problem of hunger. And meaning. And meaning only comes from myth.

Reclaiming Myth

Science is based on measurement and mathematics. Technology tries to make life efficient, productive, predictable and controllable. However, emotions cannot be measured, quantified or regulated. In other words, emotions are outside the scope of science. No science can explain why modern nation states need borders to restrict the movement of people, or why there exist hierarchies amongst the most educated. The arguments offered are always subjective, and rather silly.

Rather than admitting this, scientists simply ignored emotions and mocked psychology (the study of the human mind) as pseudoscience. At most, neuroscience is used to study mental responses in the best universities to create addictive-technology that amplifies dopamine addiction and generates vast profit, 'ethically'.

Humans express emotions through literature, art and theatre. They present concepts of the mind using metaphors (the use of familiar words to communicate the unfamiliar). Every tribe in the world is unique not just because of its technology but because of its stories, symbols and rituals. These were created by older generations to manage the hungers, fears and curiosities of the younger generations of the tribe. These had to be trusted if the tribe wished to survive. If the tribe survived, the individual survived. To prevent disruption, new ideas were seen as threats; old ideas

A Trap and an Escape

and elder folk were trusted. Myths constructed beliefs that got communities to behave in a particular way that ensured their survival over thousands of years.

For the last 200 years, myth has been used as a synonym for fiction and fantasy, because scientists failed to appreciate the metaphor. They took everything literally. In the last few decades, more and more scholars are separating fantasies and fictions meant for entertainment, expression, reflection and propaganda from myths transmitted over generations that communicate cultural truths and transform a people into a community.

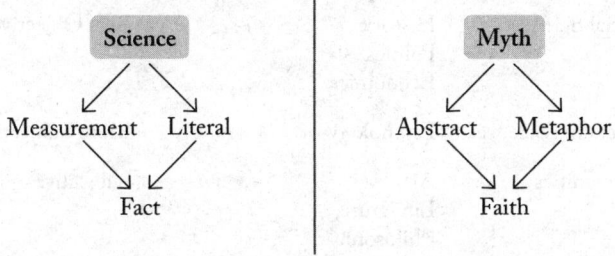

Today, mythology is no longer the study of falsehoods peddled by savages. Myth is distinguished from other forms of storytelling. The point of myth is not to entertain or educate or influence. It is to give the world a structure in which humans can find identity and meaning. It answers questions that are outside the scope of science. Science answers how, not why. Why do we exist? Who is pure and who is impure? What happens after we die? The answers are cultural, expressed in stories, rituals and symbols. These bind a community. Modern nation states have national myths for this reason – which bind citizens, get them infuriated when their flags are burnt or their borders violated. Like ancient tribes, we still fight over hunting grounds, share of harvests and control over women's reproductive organs. There is nothing rational about it, despite the complex logical arguments or the presentation of facts.

Type of Subject	Subjects	Measurement	Knowledge
Earth Sciences	Physics, Chemistry, Biology	++++++	Objective
Social Sciences	History, Politics, Economics	+++	Less Objective
(Pseudo?) Sciences	Psychology	+	More Subjective
Humanities	Art, Literature, Philosophy	–	Subjective

The failure of science to understand the human mind meant that rationalists and scientists saw myths as propaganda tools to control and manipulate the human mind. Stories, symbols and rituals were just meant to brainwash people to buy goods and services and follow a particular political ideology. Even today, intellectuals see themselves as rational, logical, scientific people who do not need myth. And yet, without myth, they have no identity, no explanation for

why they matter, why they exist, why they should be taken seriously by anyone. So they have spawned 'enlightened' atheistic myths such as:
- Capitalism (achievement-based identity)
- Socialism (justice-based identity)
- Libertarianism (individual-based identity, free of state control)

Any student of mythology can see these 'atheistic' myths follow the same structure as that of ancient Western myth:
- The Greek myth of individual struggles and heroic achievement
- The Islamic myth of martyrdom in the quest to institute laws of the one true god

Logical Statement from West	Mythical Statement from West
State is impersonal and fair	God is just
Follow state laws	Obey God's laws
Patriotism	Devotion
Traitor	Infidel
Died speaking truth to power	Martyr
Fascist	Devil
Entrepreneur	Hero
Privileged	Olympian gods
Successful	Elysium, afterlife of the memorable ones
Oppressed	Tartarus, afterlife of endless repetitive meaningless tasks
Middle Class	Asphodel, afterlife of mediocrity

The reason why the West does not see Islam as a Western myth is because the West defines itself on the basis of the eastern and western halves of the Roman Empire. Every Western nomenclature is rooted in its own imagination of itself. The rest of the world does not carry that burden. To understand modern society, we need to understand Western myth better, and for that, we have to distinguish Western myth from Eastern myth and both from Indian myth.

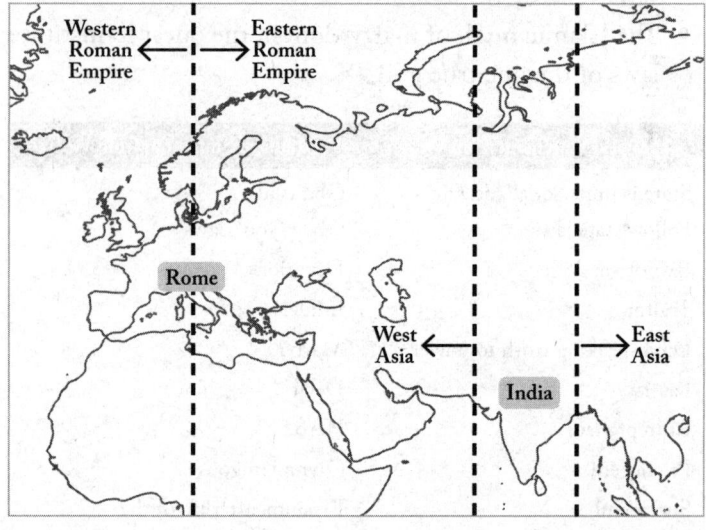

Where is the West?

A Trap and an Escape

West Is Not East Is Not India

While there are as many myths as there are cultures, we can group them into three major groups for the sake of the ideas in this book:

- **Western myth:** that only one universal 'truth' governs this world. In pre-modern Euro-America, this truth was religion; in modern Euro-America, this was science; in postmodern Euro-America, it is the woke anarchy of postmodern theorists. These are cultures that love to argue and convert others to their way of thinking. Western myth also shapes the Islamic world, which resists Euro-American values. It is all about justice.
- **Eastern myth:** that a wall separates nature from culture, the civilized from the savage. This is a culture that is at peace with borders and hierarchies, as that creates order. Hence, the Great Wall and the Firewall of China, the hermit kingdoms of Korea and the expressionless faces of Japan.
- **Indian myth:** that all myths are valid, contextual, dynamic, relevant to some and interconnected with others. This is the culture where the invisible mind is as valid as the visible body, where the present life cannot ignore the influence of past lives and the impact on future lives. Subjective peace matters here far more than truth, order, the good life or the winning argument.

Escape the Bakasura Trap

Type of Subject	West	India	East
Individual-focused mythology	Hero	Hermit	Sage
Group-focused mythology	Judge	Household	Emperor

Great civilizations typically have an in-built feedback loop to prevent excess, much like how Capitalism that favours the individual and wealth-generation is balanced by Socialism that favours the group and wealth-distribution. In the West, Greek myths of heroes defying the Olympian gods were challenged by Mesopotamian, and later Biblical, myths that favoured submission to transcendental authority. The Eastern world had no belief in the transcendent. It valued nature, and like in nature, every species respected the alpha: the child bowed to the parent, the young bowed to the old, the woman bowed to the man, the subordinate to the boss. But this was challenged by Taoist monks who saw everything as fluid, not fixed. Unlike the West where humans were privileged, the East saw humans as part of nature. Neither West nor East valued the mind as much as India's monks did. Whose imagination mattered? The hermit went inwards, expanding his own truth. The hermit went outwards, valuing other people's truths too.

A Trap and an Escape

The privileging of science over myth in the last two centuries has much to do with the fact that science emerged in the Western world based on the myth of one truth. This is the reason we find Euro-American politics constantly swinging between extremes: atheism and fanaticism, pursuit of profit and social justice, individualism and collectivism. If we break the spell of one truth, we can accommodate science alongside various cultural truths, expressed in myth. We can locate all ideas as part of an interconnected ecosystem. We can figure out what we have in common with others and what makes us unique, and how we can work together. We can also understand how different cultures complement each other.

Western myth tends to universalize. Eastern myth tends to centralize. Indian myth widens the perspective. If Western myth talks about creating the good life in the right way, Eastern myth tells us about respecting the boundaries and rules of a system, and Indian myth tells us how everyone that consumes also eventually gets consumed. If Western myth draws attention to oppressors and the oppressed, Eastern myth draws attention to the role of authority in preventing imbalance, and Indian myth ensures we recognize that villains always see themselves as victims. If Western myth privileges culture, Eastern myth values nature and Indian myth pays attention to the mind. Western myth assumes only one culture matters, Eastern myth reminds us not to ignore nature, and Indian myth shows us how infinite human minds create finite cultures in the one nature that we all experience.

Escape the Bakasura Trap

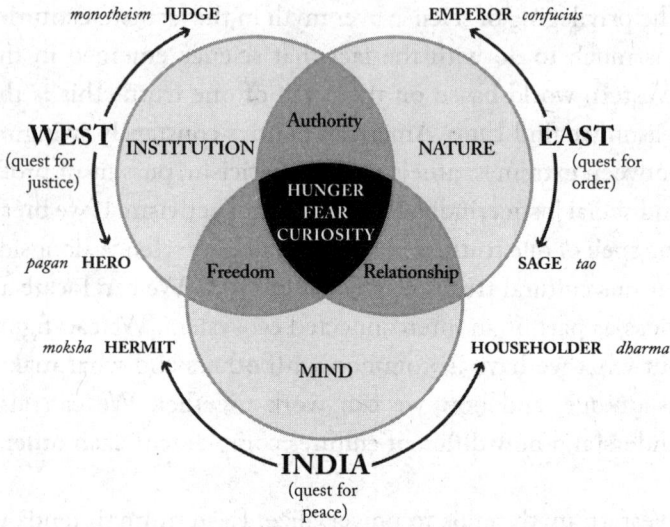

How myth unites and divides the world

> All humans are bound by hunger, fear and curiosity. In its quest for justice, West values impersonal institution over nature. In its quest for order, East values domestication of nature, and sacrifices freedom. In its quest for peace, India values the mind over nature and culture. The West is therefore torn between the individual hero and the judge of the collective; the East struggles between the Emperor's rituals and the sage's fluidity; India is torn between the hermit mindset and the housekeeper mindset, which are both invisible. No myth, no culture, has all answers.

The Modern Myth of Success

What unites humanity is the myth of paradise and hell. The word 'paradise' comes from the idea of the royal Persian walled garden, located in the middle of drylands, filled with fragrant flowers and succulent fruit. The word 'hell' comes from Hel, the goddess of the dead in Norse mythology, whose land is cold, dark, still and sterile.

Paradise is the realm with endless amounts of food. It is the realm of winners, the successful, the lucky, the faithful, the Chosen Ones. Hell is the realm of hunger, for losers, for failures, for the lucky, the unfaithful, the faithless, the infidels. Those who enjoy paradise are the gods; those who suffer hell are the demons. Humans naturally choose gods over demons. Everyone seeks food, not hunger.

- In the Greek myths, those who anger the gods are cast into hell.
- In Norse myth, cold creatures of hell threaten the warmth of paradise constantly.
- In Sumerian myth, a paradise of leisure is created for the gods by the labour of humans.
- In Egyptian myth, paradise is maintained as long as one serves the pharaoh.
- In Islamic myth, paradise is for rule-followers and hell for rule-breakers.
- In Christian myth, paradise is for those who accept Jesus as the saviour.

- In Eastern myth, paradise is order, the outcome of domestication, which makes walls and hierarchy functionally necessary.
- In Indian myth, paradise is for those who were eaten in previous lives; hell is for those who ate in previous lives.

While Western myth sees success as achievement, guided by supernatural beings such as gods and angels – now science and technology – Eastern myth views success as stability and order guided by ancestors and sages.

Western myth loves breaking boundaries and being universal, Eastern myth limits its scope to its people. Indian myth is different. It speaks of rebirth, to account for all kinds of natural and cultural diversity and dynamism.

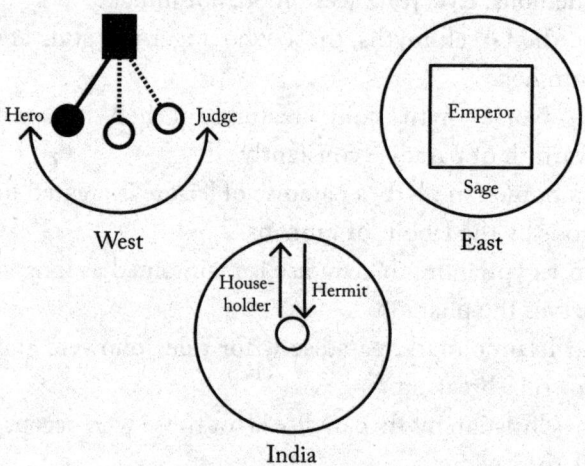

Tensions in the East, West and India

A Trap and an Escape

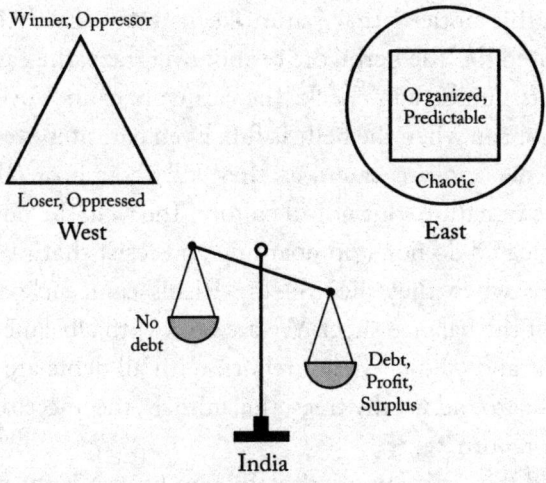

Notions of success

Indian sages – the Rishis – pondered whether paradise is meant for the successful predator who kills, or the successful prey who escapes. Is the predator a villain? Is the prey a victim? The predator does not choose to be hungry. It does not want to kill. It has no choice. It is driven by instinct. Someone has to die if the predator has to live. Is there justice for the prey that is consumed? What about justice for the predator that fails to catch a prey? Are herbivores in paradise as they have food everywhere? Or are they in hell as they cannot overeat, as then they will be too heavy to run from predators? Are carnivores in hell as they have to hunt every day for food? Or are they in heaven as they are not hunted? The Rishis refused to judge.

Escape the Bakasura Trap

The Rishis noticed that nature keeps score. Everything is accounted for. The herbivore cannot overgraze; the carnivore keeps its numbers in check. The carnivore cannot overhunt; it cannot run when the belly is full. Even parasites eventually starve, die and are eaten, as they kill their host. There is balance in nature. But not in culture. The rich, the powerful, the educated do not stop hoarding and resist sharing. What happens when they die? So the Rishis came up with the myth of the balance sheet. We are born with a balance sheet of debit and credit. We are reborn until all debts are repaid to those around us: the trees, the animals, the ancestors who will be reborn.

- Buddhist and Jain mythology says heaven is for hermits who have outgrown hunger and fear, and so they have peace, with no need for prosperity. Thus, they step away from the Rana-Bhoomi, the war zone between hell and paradise.
- Hindu mythology speaks of a heaven of householders, where everyone pays attention to the other's hunger, where everyone feeds and is fed, creating Ranga-Bhoomi, the stage of delight, where generosity and resilience create prosperity and peace for all.

A Trap and an Escape

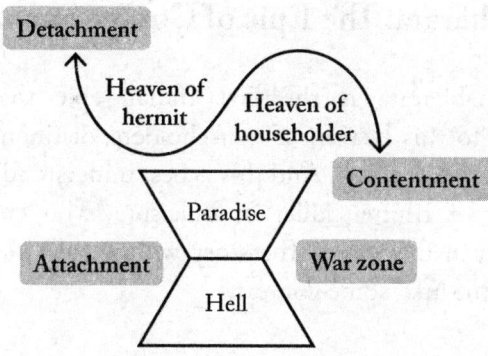

Architecture of the Indian mythic world

These ideas were first presented as Vedic poetry, then as Brahmana-Aranyaka rituals and Upanishad dialogues, and finally as stories such as the epic Mahabharata. Superficially, the Mahabharata seems like a book of war, about achievements, about winners and losers. But it is, at a deeper level, about escaping the trap of consumption and finding contentment.

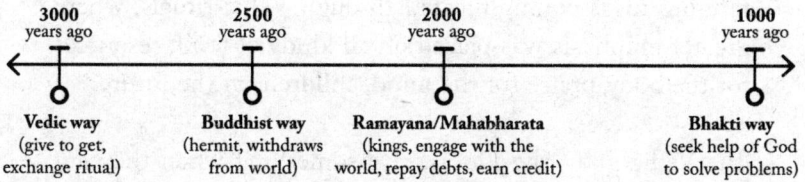

Timeline of Indian thought

Mahabharata: The Epic of Contentment

The Mahabharata is the first Indian epic that draws attention to this heaven of householders, distinguishing it from paradise and hell. And this is best understood through the story of Bhima, killer of Bakasura, who encounters Hanuman in the forest. The story will be told in the next chapter. But first, some context.

Hindus worship Hanuman as a god, because he solves problems. But he is different from a Deva, commonly translated as 'god' in English. The Devas are hungry for pleasure and leisure – they fight for paradise. They appear in the earliest layer of Hindu mythology, in the 3,000-year-old Vedas. But Hanuman belongs to a different class of deities who appear in later layers of Hindu mythology, in the 2,000-year-old epics like the Ramayana and the Mahabharata. In the thousand years in between, India saw the rise of philosophies such as the Upanishads, Buddhism and Jainism that spoke of suffering caused by hunger, thereby refining ideas communicated through Vedic rituals, where greater emphasis was placed on all kinds of food: resources for the body, praise for the mind, children for the future.

The Vedic gods, the Devas, give something when they get something. Hanuman, by contrast, does not seek anything. Though mighty, he is neither ambitious nor dominating. He is gentle and wise, attributes born of contentment. He is also immortal and therefore has knowledge of those who inhabited

A Trap and an Escape

an earlier story retold in another epic, the Ramayana. That epic, which predates events in the Mahabharata, speaks of Ram-Rajya, the perfect kingdom of Ram, where there is prosperity, pleasure and peace for all. Ram is Vishnu on earth, an avatar, a finite manifestation of the infinite divine. The people of Ram-Rajya have everything but that does not stop them from gossiping about their queen's character, which compels Ram to abandon her to protect the royal reputation. Ram's wife Sita lives with her children in the forest, while Ram's subjects enjoy Ram-Rajya judging Ram for abandoning his wife rather than defending her.

Hanuman wonders why Ram does not change the minds of his people, convince them about Sita's fidelity and purity. Must the unfaithful and impure be abandoned? That is what Ram asks Hanuman with a smile. Despite having everything why were his subjects so cruel, especially towards the king? Actions are not to be justified or condemned. They have to be understood. Even Vishnu on earth cannot control people's minds, their hungers, their fears, their curiosities. He can only do his duty as king, prioritize royal reputation as expected, than personal life. The mission to domesticate other people's minds always fails. Hanuman is asked to stay on earth and witness this.

Bakasura, Bhima and Hanuman are all born in the forest. Baka stays in the forest. Bhima moves into a human settlement. Hanuman encounters human culture but stays away from it. Baka focuses on finding food and eats everyone around him, even those who feed him. Bhima learns the value of feeding after an encounter with Hanuman. Hanuman eats fruits to sustain himself but rejects pearls to adorn himself. Baka is a metaphor for the raw human imagination coping with the limitations of nature. Bhima is a metaphor for the contracted human imagination seeking solutions in culture. Hanuman is a metaphor for the expanded human imagination that has a perspective of nature as well as culture, on the potential and limitations of science as well as myth. Many see him as a form of Shiva, a Yogi, one who has conquered hunger but who, guided by the Goddess (Sita in Hanuman's case), learns to empathize with the hungry, the Bhogi. The point of this myth is not justice, or order, but peace. Peace with the realities of nature, and culture, and the limitations of the human mind.

	Bakasura	Bhima	Hanuman
Hunger	Yes	Yes	No
Seeks Food	Yes	Yes	No
Provides Food	No	Yes	No
Evokes Curiosity	No	No	Yes

These characters are clearly fantastic vehicles of very powerful ancient ideas. We get access to them through myths, not science, as science can never ever make sense of metaphor. Subjective truth can never be measured.

A Trap and an Escape

Three Steps to Escape

This book is all about decoding metaphors and reclaiming cultural concepts. For this, we will primarily focus on stories of Bhima, as narrated in the Mahabharata, and use them to map the path from Rana-Bhoomi (where hunger fuels material growth) to Ranga-Bhoomi (where contentment fuels mental growth that accelerates material growth).

This path has three steps:
1. Eat better, by consuming more knowledge than wealth and power.
2. Kill less, by gaining insight into how food production is violent.
3. Feed more, by reflecting on who we choose to feed and who we choose to eat.

This path can be imagined in another way. It is about bettering:
1. Our 'business' body, what we seek as targets: wealth, power, knowledge, known in Hindu mythology as three goddesses viz., Lakshmi, Durga and Saraswati.
2. Our 'behavioural' body, how we do our tasks: extract, exchange, evaluate, ritually described as bali (offering sacrifice), yagna (giving to receive) and tula (weighing on the pan balance).
3. Our 'belief' body, why we track what we track: because we are dependent like Brahma, independent as Shiva and dependable like Vishnu.

Escape the Bakasura Trap

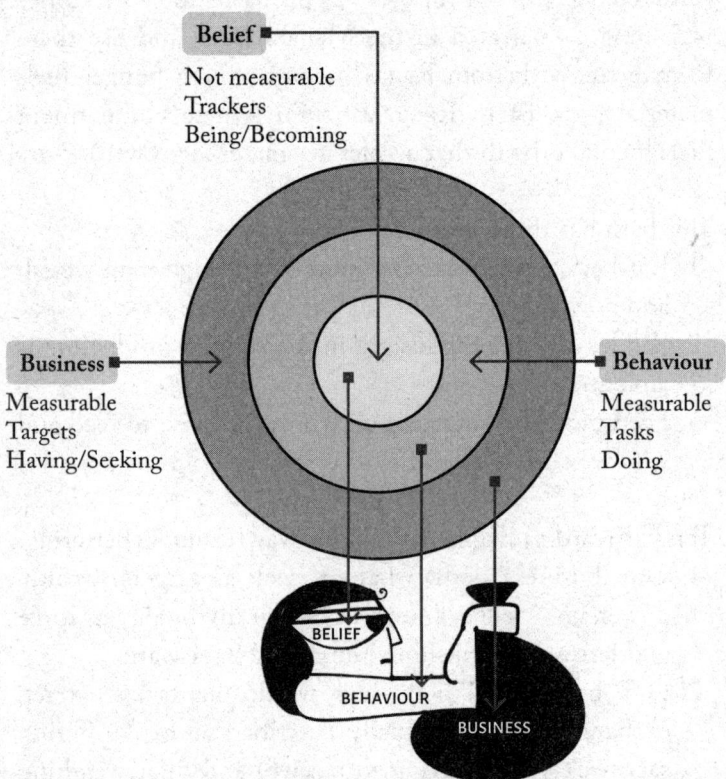

The three bodies

A Trap and an Escape

Notice how the 'belief' body is expressed in Hindu mythology using male forms (gods), while the 'business' body is constituted by female forms (goddesses). The 'behavioural' body is full of genderless verbs. These are metaphors to indicate how business and belief complement each other, like women and men, and how nouns cannot exist without verbs just as nothing can happen without behaviour. Do not let the grammar and genders distract you from the meaning.

This path is visually represented by three bricks, each with three flowers, each with five petals. The brick is the step, the flower is the sub-set, and the petals are the individual ideas.

This path does not end with a climax; it is circular. The end of Step 3 should ideally make you return to Step 1. So you refine your understanding, churning your mind with new frameworks to appreciate the world.

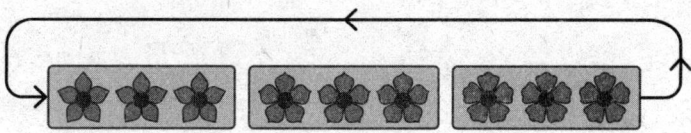

Escape the Bakasura Trap

The ideas in this book do not seek to replace what you already know. They seek to expand your mind with new ideas, enabling you to supplement, complement, reinforce, amplify, dilute or substitute what you already know. So engage with this book in the spirit of curiosity, not combat, keeping in mind:

Within infinite myths lies an eternal truth.
Who sees it all?
Varuna has but a thousand eyes
Indra, a hundred
You and I only two.

A Trap and an Escape

Map of Three Steps Towards Contentment

1. Eat Better, to Nourish Your 'Business' Body		
Wealth (Lakshmi)	**Power (Durga)**	**Knowledge (Saraswati)**
Pleasure	Toolkit	Ideas
Excess	Insider	Curriculum
Novelty	Superior	Transmission
Unique	Free	Filter
Carry Forward	Immortal	Memories
2. Kill Less, to Retrain Your 'Behavioural' Body		
Extraction (Bali)	**Exchange (Yagna)**	**Evaluation (Tula)**
Resources	Receive	Agreement
Labour	Obligation	Customization
Share	Popularity	Gamification
Justice	Network	Luck
Justification	Relationships	Branding
3. Feed More, to Sensitize Your 'Belief' Body		
Dependent (Brahma)	**Independent (Shiva)**	**Dependable (Vishnu)**
Domesticated	Restrained	Playacting
Quarrels	Indifferent	Repay
Successful	Opportunist	Reclaim
Helpless	Paranoid	Reinvest
Exiled	Empathy	Desirability

Step 1 of 3: Eat Better, to Nourish Your 'Business' Body

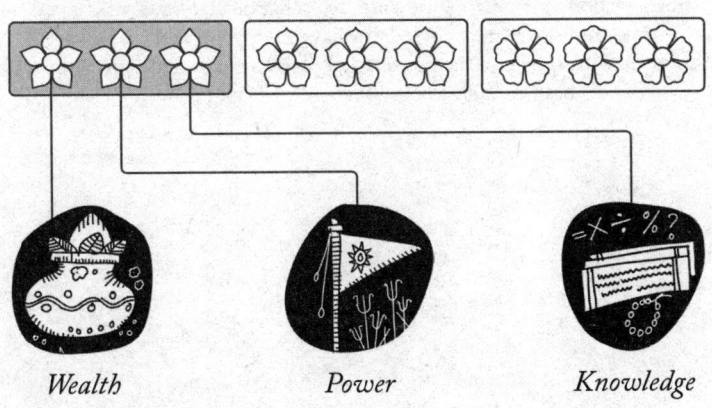

Wealth *Power* *Knowledge*

Business body = The target of your life. What do you have/seek/hoard? To be admired, feared, envied? To have more than others? To have sufficient? To consume the most out of life? To get more to give others? To have enough to be able to give without counting?

Bhima meets Hanuman

It all began in a forest. Both Baka and Bhima were born here. Both were hungry all the time. Both had to forage for food. Baka would eat everything and everyone that was edible. Bhima would digest food so quickly that he always appeared hungry, earning the nickname of Vrik-odara, or wolf-bellied.

Baka never left the forest. Bhima was taken to his uncle's palace shortly after his father's death. There he was nourished, protected and educated. Bhima grew up an entitled prince as his late father, Pandu, was a king. Pandu had two wives: Kunti and Madri. Bhima was Kunti's middle child, the second of her three sons. He had two young stepbrothers, the twin sons of Madri.

Pandu had withdrawn to the forest on learning he could never make his wives pregnant. However, in the forest, sages told him about the code of culture that enabled a childless man to obtain sons by adopting the wife's children. Thus, the sons of Kunti and Madri, born of different fathers, were declared Pandu's sons, the Pandavas. They would inherit Pandu's property, his crown, his estates, his titles.

When Pandu and Madri died, Kunti took the Pandavas to Pandu's palace to secure their royal inheritance. There they were met with hostility. Pandu's blind elder brother, Dhritarashtra, and his hundred sons, the Kauravas, resented the idea of having to share the family wealth with them. They saw the Pandavas as rivals, imposters and pretenders. Their hatred amplified when they realized the Pandavas were far more talented than they were, winning the admiration of their tutor, Drona, when they successfully conquered and split the kingdom of Panchala into two, giving one half to Drona. They tried to kill Bhima by poisoning his food. It only made him stronger. They tried to drown him. But he survived. Finally, they set the Pandava house on fire, forcing the five brothers and their mother to run and take refuge in the forest. That is where Bhima encountered Baka.

Step 1 of 3: Eat Better, to Nourish Your 'Business' Body

Baka terrorized everyone in the forest. He ate their food and even those who fed him. He ate everything and everyone. Bhima killed him and made the forest safe. He killed other demons too. In exchange, the people of the forest gave him food. Finally, a woman called Hidimbi offered to be Bhima's wife, protect and provide for Bhima and his family, provided he stopped killing her hungry brothers, the so-called Asuras, maligned by all as demons. Bhima agreed. Life was good in the forest, thanks to Hidimbi. There was prosperity and peace. There was pleasure and there was leisure.

But Kunti was restless. She reminded her sons that they were obliged to be the kings their father wanted them to be. So Bhima's younger brother, Arjuna, won a princess called Draupadi in an archery competition. On Kunti's instruction, Draupadi was made the common wife of the Pandava brothers, to be shared equally. This marriage gave the Pandavas a powerful father-in-law. It gave them the courage to return to their uncle's house and demand their share of the family property.

The Pandavas were given the underdeveloped half of the inheritance, a forest. Arjuna set the forest aflame, killed all its inhabitants and cleared a land where the Pandavas established a city called Indraprastha. To make Indraprastha sovereign, Bhima killed

Escape the Bakasura Trap

Jarasandha, the tyrant, who terrorized all kings for tribute.

Though each of the five Pandava brothers had equal rights to the kingdom, as they had only their wife, Yudhishthira was crowned king as he was the eldest. Everyone had to obey him without question. So Bhima could say nothing when Yudhishthira wagered the family fortune in a gambling match and, to everyone's horror, lost the game, forfeiting Pandava rights over the kingdom as well as their own bodies. Bhima was told to restrain himself as he watched the Kauravas publicly humiliating his wife by dragging her by her hair, claiming her as a maid. They were breaking no rules. They had won a slave and were free to do with her as they pleased. To make peace, it was decided that the Pandavas could reclaim their land after thirteen years. Until then, they had to wander in the forest like homeless exiles.

It was during this period in the forest that Bhima encountered Hanuman. The wind brought with it a flower that made Draupadi smile. Bhima decided to fetch more such flowers for her. He began walking against the wind that had carried the flower, determined to locate its source. He walked straight, shoving away all plants and animals that came in his path, terrorizing all with his determination and focus. But then he stumbled on a frail old monkey. Irritated,

Step 1 of 3: Eat Better, to Nourish Your 'Business' Body

> Bhima tried to kick the monkey aside, only to discover that he could not even move its tail. A humbled Bhima realized he was in the presence of Hanuman, the mightiest, gentlest and wisest of all forest creatures.
>
> Kunti had told Bhima that his father was the wind god. That made Hanuman his half-brother, as they shared a common father. A fragrant wind, carrying a lotus, had brought these sons of the wind god together. Hanuman asked Bhima why he was treating the creatures of the forest with such disrespect. Was it because he had been stripped of all dignity by the Kauravas? Was it because he felt powerless before his elder brother, Yudhishthira? Was it to impress his wife, Draupadi, and upstage his younger brother, Arjuna?
>
> No one had ever asked Bhima such questions. Not his brothers, his mother, his wife or his teachers. Find the answers, said Hanuman, and you will find contentment and be at peace.

Bhima suddenly became aware of the many hungers around him. Baka looked at everyone around either as food or rival. There was the Kaurava hunger that prevented them from sharing anything. Drona's hunger for revenge, for a past humiliation. Kunti's hunger for her children's inheritance. Pandava hunger for Draupadi, restrained by rules that forced everyone to give equal measure to those younger and those elder. Yudhishthira's hunger for risks in the gambling hall, just to feel that momentary rush of victory. Arjuna's hunger to be better. Duryodhana's hunger to humiliate his cousins, finding ways to do so legitimately. His own hunger for revenge, for justice, for Kunti's approval, Yudhishthira's gratitude, Draupadi's admiration, Arjuna's envy. Focused on his own hunger, he had not seen how he had terrified the plants and animals of the forest. He, who always sought food, and took his power for granted, now sought knowledge. Hanuman had nudged him to eat better.

Bhima realized he was different from plants and animals. Plants and animals have only one body that they take with them wherever they go. He had an additional layer: property! Even if he did not carry it physically, it was there with him all the time. Not just his clothes and adornments, but also his estates, his assets, his titles, his weapons, his tools, his skills, his knowledge. Not everything was visible, but he carried everything all the time with him, assuming everyone saw them, and made way for him in the forest, as they did in the palace. This was his 'business' body. It had three constituents, visualized by the Rishis as three goddesses:

A. The **wealth** that helped Bhima live the good life was visualized as the pot-holding goddess known as Lakshmi, surrounded by lotuses and elephants.

B. The **power** that made Bhima fearsome and secured him respect was visualized as the trident-holding, tiger-riding goddess known as Durga.

Step 1 of 3: Eat Better, to Nourish Your 'Business' Body

C. The **knowledge** that enabled Bhima to enhance his capabilities and grow as a person was visualized as the lute-holding, goose-riding goddess known as Saraswati.

In this section, our first of three steps, we explore the 'business' body that is constituted by everything we have, seek, grab, hoard, exchange, give and receive. We need to appreciate how success in modern society is about chasing Lakshmi and Durga and reducing Saraswati to wealth-generating skills and power-generating hacks. It has nothing to do with understanding our hunger or fear, or witnessing our lack of curiosity.

Business ▶ **Wealth**

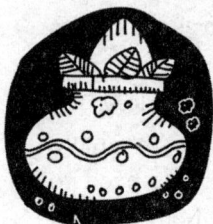

Sunlight is food for plants. They grow leaves to collect it. Leaves are food for herbivores. They seek it out. Flesh is food for carnivores. They hunt for it. Human food is complex. We want more than just nutrients. What we seek is not just kept within the body. It is collected outside too.

i. We seek **pleasure**. We invent new ways to indulge our senses, release endorphins and dopamine.
ii. We imagine scarcity and so hoard money, which holds the promise of future pleasure. There is pleasure in hoarding **surplus**.
iii. We get bored easily, so seek **novelty** and variety over quantity and quality.
iv. Our consumption is not just determined by our biology. It is also cultural. It is imaginative. It differentiates us from other humans. Makes us **unique**.
v. We compete all our lives to have more than others and wonder if this hunger is **carried forward** to the next life, if there is one.

The word 'lakshmi' is derived from 'laksh' which means 'target'. Lakshmi is undoubtedly the most sought-after goddess of our 'business' body. She holds the promise of pleasure and leisure, of comfort, but never contentment.

Step 1 of 3: Eat Better, to Nourish Your 'Business' Body

Business ▶ Wealth ▶ **Pleasure**

Plants seek nutrients. So they produce leaves and roots that move towards sunlight and water. Animals seek nutrients. So herbivores seek pastures where they gather plant flesh while carnivores hunt as they seek animal flesh. Humans seek nutrients and much more. We seek pleasure, through our eyes, ears, nose, tongue, skin and for our mind. We seek beauty, music, aromas and perfumes, tastes, texture and delight. So we seek cuisines, clothing, shelter, entertainment, transport.

We do not adapt to our ecosystem as plants and animals do, we adapt our ecosystem to our needs until it brings pleasure. We get creative. We domesticate and cultivate culture to our needs and tastes to establish culture. We see nature as resources to be processed and refined till it grants us pleasure. We do not see trees; we see wood. We do not see sheep; we see wool and mutton. We do not see humans; we see labour.

By outsourcing labour, we can combine pleasure with leisure. Get everything we want without effort. We strive to recreate the paradise we experienced when we were infants, and all our needs were met by our parents.

> **What do you crave in a snack: nutrition or taste? Do not lie.**

Escape the Bakasura Trap

Business ▶ Wealth ▶ **Surplus**

There is a natural limit to the hunger of plants and animals. Plants do not grow endlessly. The herbivore will not graze endlessly. The carnivore will not hunt endlessly. Overeating prey get hunted easily. Parasites die when they kill their hosts. But humans have managed to overeat and hoard and still survive, using innovation.

We wear one dress but can keep several more in the closet for future use. We use one car but can keep a dozen more in the garage for future use. Our creativity expands with our desires. Both creativity and desire are fuelled by imagination. Our hunger is amplified as we can envisage future scarcity and future abundance. Nightmares of scarcity fill us with dread.

Dreams of abundance fill us with comfort. We shun the former and seek the latter: more food, more clothes, more houses, more entertainment, more transport, more resources, more discoveries, more inventions. There is no limit to how much we can seek, consume and hoard.

> Do you know what is the minimum wage in our country? What can be the maximum wage for the maximum luxury?

To make things easier to store, humans invented money, a symbol which can be exchanged for whatever resources we seek. We can store this symbolic wealth in many ways: First it was shells, then coins, then paper, then cards, now it is

Step 1 of 3: Eat Better, to Nourish Your 'Business' Body

stored as numbers in a database. That is how we now have humans with trillions, who continue to crave for more. We have innovated efficient ways of storing hoarded wealth that will never be actually consumed.

Business ▶ Wealth ▶ **Novelty**

Humans get bored easily. So we constantly need new ways to arouse our senses and entertain our minds. We seek refinement, better goods, better services, more efficient, more effective. We seek novelty, variety, new things, more things, more choices. So we create markets where we can exchange goods and get more options.

In markets we get goods and services from faraway places, from mountains, rivers, deserts, islands. Driven by whims, we have sought resources in almost every geography, establishing homes in all ecosystems, from the Arctic to the equator and beyond, discovering new homelands, inventing new ways of harnessing resources.

Pleasures shift with availability. Goods and services flood markets, with supply creating demand. The desire for fashion increases as boutiques offer more novelty and variety. Marketing is about making you want things you do not need, and what you cannot afford. The more food we see, the hungrier we get. This adds to human hunger and the quest for food. Now we can order online and get deliveries at home, and secure products from every corner of the world with ease. Hungers are being thus amplified.

> Do you know a friend who is constantly seeking something that no one else has? Why?

Step 1 of 3: Eat Better, to Nourish Your 'Business' Body

We eagerly await how indulgences can get better. Stability is boring. Humans also seek the rare, exclusive access to stuff that is out of reach for others. Rarity and exclusivity make us feel special. We want that wedding gown that no one else will wear, or the design that will never be duplicated. We thus express our limitless yearning to feel special through consumption.

Business ▶ Wealth ▶ Uniqueness

Not all human cravings are biologically determined. Some are culturally conditioned; they help us be part of a group. Others are private yearnings; these make us unique individuals. Needs are what help us survive. Pleasure is what we want. Luxuries are that which we demand to establish status.

Pleasures shift with age: What we seek in our teenage years does not comfort us in old age.

Pleasures shift with culture: Music and dance from one culture does not always appeal to those from other cultures. Jade is precious in China, not India, so much sought-after by Chinese tycoons, not Indian tycoons. Since different cultures seek different kinds of food, humans need to establish different kinds of kitchens to satisfy different demands.

Religion also shapes our hunger, tells us what to eat and what not to eat. Muslims seek halal food. Jews seek kosher food. Muslim women wear veils to cover the head and face. They are indulgences, not necessary for survival, but important to integrate into society. Then there are personal hungers, for the satisfaction of the self, yearnings that are neither necessary for survival, nor endorsed by culture, like cross-dressing or drug-taking.

Step 1 of 3: Eat Better, to Nourish Your 'Business' Body

Hobbyists and hoarders are satisfying emotional needs not seen in plants and animals. A dog buries bones to chew at leisure, but we cannot give any purpose to the act of collecting stamps or plastic cups. Our sense of self is nourished by our private pursuits – our customized desires.

All humans need food, clothing and shelter. But only Muslims need mosques and the Japanese need sushi. And all of us have that one hunger that is unique to us, and for which we seek no companion. That hunger reminds us we are different, unique, not part of a herd or pack or hive.

> **Do you like personalized branding of luxury items? Why?**

Escape the Bakasura Trap

Business ▶ Wealth ▶ **Carry Forward**

When we die, we leave behind all the resources we hoarded. But we do not want to. In tombs across Egypt, Eurasia and Mesopotamia, we find humans buried with their favourite food, clothes, tools, spouses, slaves, pets, furniture, carts and boats. This is meant to satisfy their hunger in the afterlife. In China, one burns paper money so that the ancestors can use it for their needs in the land of the dead. Hindu funeral rituals are all about feeding the dead as they await rebirth.

These practices are a reminder that humans can imagine hunger persisting after death. This hunger is what turns the dead into ghosts. Their unfulfilled yearnings make them haunt the living. These stories of unhappy souls fuel our desire to be fulfilled in this life. Ghost stories frighten us. They remind us that a life well lived is true success. Those who die in peace, having burped in satisfaction, will not trouble the living for more food.

> If you had a tomb, what would you take with you to the afterlife? What would your sibling carry?

In the Valmiki Ramayana, there is a story of Shveta, who attains paradise after he dies as he lived a very pious life. But in paradise, he is still hungry. So he is forced to return to the land of the living each day looking for food. There is no one to feed him on earth as he fed no one when he was alive. So

Step 1 of 3: Eat Better, to Nourish Your 'Business' Body

Shveta is forced to eat his own corpse, that regenerates itself daily, the result of his having lived a pious life. It was not enough that he was a pious man, with little use for wealth. He had not been a generous man. He had not generated surplus for feeding others. And so he suffered hunger even after attaining paradise.

Business ▶ Power

We cannot see the hunger of plants and animals, but we can see their quest for food. We cannot see fear, but we can see the bark and thorn of plants, hear the hiss of the serpent, the snort of the bull, the growl of the dog and feel the sting of the bee. Humans are frightened too. But unlike plants and animals, we have found ways to hoard power, be more capable than our physical body allows us to be.

i. We have developed **tools** to improve our capability and capacity, our productivity. Tools become weapons to secure food procured. Language enables humans to engage with other humans, give meaning and mobilize gangs.

ii. We share our toolkit with **insiders**. We establish borders to keep away outsiders. Humans create bands, tribes, clans, just like animals have herds, hives and packs. But ours is based on choice and tradition, not biology.

iii. Within the group we erect hierarchies to define those who are **inferior**, who get the smaller share of food.

iv. While we like using power to control others, we do not like others using power to control us. So we seek **freedom**, either in society, or from society, from nature even.

Step 1 of 3: Eat Better, to Nourish Your 'Business' Body

v. We create tools to combat death even. Find tricks like inheritance to outsmart death, be **immortal**, at least in our own imagination.

This chapter is about Durga, who makes us feel safe and significant. More often than not our quest for Lakshmi is actually a quest for Durga. We will be powerful when we are rich. But the rich know that the truly powerful need not be rich. The word 'durga' is derived from 'durg' which means 'fortress', indicating she is critical for peace. But she is not enough for contentment.

Business ▶ Power ▶ **Toolkit**

We need power to secure food. We also need power to prevent our food from being stolen and to protect ourselves from becoming food. The leaves and roots of plants help them get food; thorns and bark keep away grazers. Herbivores have hooves to run towards pasture and away from prey. Carnivores have paws and claws, talons and beaks to catch prey and fight predators. The power of plants and animals is located within the body. There is nothing outside.

The human body is weak, comparatively, with no feathers, fur, scales, claws or horns. We use our imagination to invent tools that help us extract food and resources from nature. Human tools can be mental (language, or mantra), physical (skill, or tantra) and technological (instrument, or yantra).

Language allows humans to communicate abstract concepts with other humans, which is very different from the direct and descriptive communication of opportunities and threats seen between termites and bees. Language can be used to create borders. Those who do not speak our language do not belong. Language can be used to create hierarchies. Refined speech distinguishes the elite from those who speak crudely. Language can also be used to praise and insult and thus make people feel powerful or powerless. Language allows humans to gossip, transmit information and even create laws.

Step 1 of 3: Eat Better, to Nourish Your 'Business' Body

Humans can train the body to perform complex tasks like climbing trees in the neighbourhood, swim in faraway seas, ride camels, elephants and horses, shoot arrows from bows, bullets from guns, use laptops and swing lassos. Thus we create division of labour. The one who fights complements the one who cooks and cleans. Different physical bodies are trained to do different tasks. Different people think about different human problems.

Instruments amplify human capability and capacity – allowing us to melt rocks, build traps, chop trees, explode mountains, fly through air and travel over water. Instruments allow us to see better, smell better, hear better and gather more information about us. Microscopes and telescopes change our understanding of the world. Technology helps us grasp better, move faster, strike from a distance, keep information outside our body in books and databases. With computers, robots and artificial intelligence, we are seeking to create instruments which are more efficient and effective than humans in certain tasks.

> What do you carry in your travel bag to feel safe? What does your spouse carry?

Business ▶ Power ▶ **Insider**

There are no borders or fences in nature. To increase the chances of survival, animals form groups in the form of hives, herds and packs. Even plants communicate with each other through underground mycelial networks about threats and opportunities in the ecosystem. Animals also establish territories to secure their source of food. The strongest gets the territory and the mates.

Human behaviour is different. We can choose. We are not bound to follow our biological relatives. They are not biologically obliged to help us. The greatest human invention is the mental concept of 'mine'. So we have my tools, my skills, my body, my land, my livestock, my food, my weapons, my knowledge. We also have my wife, my children, my family, my tribe, my clan, my caste, my community, my nation. Humans invented laws to create these boundaries between what is mine and what is not mine. It applies to concepts, things and people.

To identify my children, we need to identify my wife. Thus came the laws of marriage, fidelity and adultery. Also laws of adoption for the childless. Humans have property, not territory. Property is created by law, not force. Property can be bequeathed to whosoever we choose, even the unworthy. Law is about restraining the strong. It is about distributing power – granting opportunities to the weak. Law is supposed

Step 1 of 3: Eat Better, to Nourish Your 'Business' Body

to increase opportunities and decrease threats to the weak. In the jungle, the big eat the small. Humans can take care of the weak and the helpless. Laws are supposed to ensure that. Laws are applied to insiders. Not outsiders.

Outsiders are kept out forcibly with weapons and walls and treaties. Those within walls are bound to follow the laws. Laws define what is mine and what is yours and so define what constitutes me and what constitutes you. Laws define our relatives and our property. Laws can be formal or informal, visible or invisible. Laws tell us what to eat, what to wear, and so distinguish ourselves and help others identify us.

With borders comes the idea of violation. When we take what is yours without consent, we break the law, we violate your sense of being, we become a thief. We feel powerful when we can expand our borders. We call it growth when what we have expands. Capitalists pursue monopoly to feel powerful. Socialists are constantly seeking to convert people to their cause of justice, like missionaries who were called 'fishers of men' – expanding the size of the tribe of believers.

Borders inform people who is to be considered friend and who is foe, who is ally and who is rival, who needs to be fed and who can be allowed to starve, who needs to be protected and who can be exploited and enslaved.

> Do you judge people by their names and surnames?
> Do you know people who change their names and surnames?

Borders are crucial to human identity. We strive to not be like our neighbours for fear we will merge with them and lose our identity. Those who speak of the annihilation of caste and fluidity of gender and nations without borders do not realize how these ideas make people insecure. There is a reason humans do not live in the forest. There is a reason for why we created borders. There is no rape in the forest, as there is no concept of property. There is no concept of property because there is no concept of border. Anyone with force can grab. The doe does not seek justice when the hyena grabs the newborn fawn as food.

Step 1 of 3: Eat Better, to Nourish Your 'Business' Body

Business ▶ Power ▶ **Superior**

Animals have a pecking order, with the alpha at the top, betas below and omegas at the bottom. Nature is dynamic, changing with age. This determines who gets how much share. In nature, the strongest gets the best share. In social animals, the oldest gets more respect as the oldest has the longest memory of food and water sources.

Human groups also have hierarchies. Who deserves more? Who deserves less? Is division based on merit, on age, on need, on desire, on age or on whim? We favour those we consider ours over the children of strangers. Some favour the eldest child, some the youngest, some the most talented. They get a greater share of attention, affection and even property.

Hierarchies are created based on what we have. The rich are higher than the poor. Those with status and strength are higher than those without. The beautiful are higher than the ugly. The talented are much more sought after than the mediocre. In a tribe, everyone does everything. Over time, clans emerge, with specialized skills. Some clans get higher status depending on how much wealth they generate, how much influence they hold on others, and how strong they are.

The Hindu caste system was based on purity – some vocations were considered purer and allowed to live near the temple, eat refined food; some were considered so polluting that they had to live in the fringes of the village and eat leftover food.

Hierarchies grant us identity, just like borders. They tell us who is above us and who is below us, who to obey and who to order, who will feed and who has to be fed. Hierarchies create predictability and stability, but they also create oppression. For those on top stay on top by pushing others down and denying them opportunities to rise. In nature, the female hyena kills the babies of her rivals to ensure her children dominate the next generation. Humans secure their place by praising those they fear and abusing those they wish to exploit.

> Which of these identities truly matter: religious, caste/tribe, linguistic, nationality, gender? Does your child agree?

We rise higher by cornering the bigger share; hence we do not care if others have been denied what they deserve. The more we have, the more we are valued. Those who do not have anything seek respect. Unlike domesticated animals, they are not just content with a regular supply of food. No one wants to be chattel, content at the bottom of the pyramid, bearing the burden of the elite.

Step 1 of 3: Eat Better, to Nourish Your 'Business' Body

Business ▶ Power ▶ **Freedom**

Plants work every day for food. Animals work every day for food. They do not rest. If they rest, they die. Humans can take holidays. Because we create surplus or because someone else labours for us. The more we have, the less we need to do. We can consume all the time, or work only if we want to on projects that interest us. That is freedom to choose that we crave for. But society does not grant us that. We are bound by family obligations, government regulations and religious expectations to function in a certain way.

Our borders, our hierarchies, designed to secure our estates and our status, end up entrapping us. We yearn for freedom without giving up our privileges. We yearn for freedom to do whatever we wish, without having to pay for it, or suffering its consequences. We seek liberty in society, be the indulged children of the rich and the powerful who can afford to do anything and who are never questioned nor disciplined no matter what they do.

But a life of indulgence comes with dependence. We depend on our resources, our power, our tools, our privileges, our relationships. We feel locked by fences we created for our own security. We feel fettered by the very laws we used to grant ourselves greater importance. The rich and the powerful feel besieged by the hungry and the frightened, who appear frightening. The lazy cannot live without servants. The leader is trapped by his followers, the teacher by his students. We are trapped by our insecurities, our fear of surprises, shocks and accidents. Insurance and assurance does not take away the fear.

The poor refuse to be oppressed and so fight revolutions to gain freedom. The rich refuse to be bullied by labour, without whom they cannot survive. Borders and hierarchies turn us into domesticated animals. Our desire to control others also entraps us.

While the West seeks freedom in society, which involves controlling others, India speaks of a different kind of freedom, from culture as well as nature, the end of social responsibilities as well as biological urges, a withdrawal from social, natural and even psychological demands. Some sages wander away. Others return to enlighten those they left behind and end up entrapping themselves in their own spiritual retreats.

> Would you feel free in a world where no one noticed you? Do you trap your friends with judgement?

Step 1 of 3: Eat Better, to Nourish Your 'Business' Body

Business ▶ Power ▶ **Immortal**

Despite all the power in the world, we cannot live forever. We have to die. We work hard to delay death, but death eventually catches up. Fear of the afterlife is used to control the way we live. We are told we will be punished if we do not live the right way, as prescribed by culture. We are told we must live in a way that does not bring shame to our ancestors. We fear what will happen to the world after us, and so we create systems that will outlive us.

We know that what we have outlives us. So we strive for immortality through possessions: family name, estates, titles and achievements. We fear we will be forgotten. Humans establish states. States establish judicial courts. Judicial courts are filled with registrars who register human relationships, property and wills. This assures what we have continues to survive long after we are dead, creating an illusion of immortality.

We hope to live on through our children who inherit our estates and our titles, even if they do not inherit our intelligence, our skills or our character. If we do not seek that immortality, we would not bother with marriage, children and inheritance.

In the *Kathasaritsagar*, a collection of ancient Indian parables, a king performs a ritual to feed his ancestors. Three hands sprout up to receive this offering. One belongs to

Escape the Bakasura Trap

> **Why do so many people die without a proper registered will? Have you made your will?**

the impotent king who married his mother, whose title he inherited. The second to the man who made the king's mother pregnant, whose genes the king inherited. The third belongs to the man who raised the king who was orphaned at an early age, from whom the king received love, knowledge and skills. Who is the true father? From whom did the king get his true inheritance?

 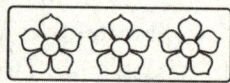 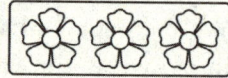

Step 1 of 3: Eat Better, to Nourish Your 'Business' Body

Business ▶ Knowledge

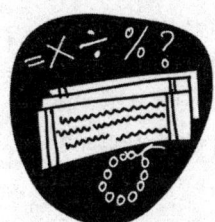

Plants and animals do not go to school. Humans do. Because we create, transmit and refine knowledge. Knowledge separates human groups as different communities have different knowledge systems, with different metaphors, and different tools for survival, in different ecosystems.

i. We are full of **ideas**. We want to improve the world. Not just react to it. Thus we create knowledge, which separates us from the rest of nature.

ii. We have an entire **curriculum** about the material world, social world, psychological world.

iii. We **transmit** our knowledge to the next generation.

iv. New knowledge threatens old knowledge. External knowledge threatens internal knowledge. So we debate and discuss, approach new ideas with fear. We **filter** out what we cannot handle.

v. We imagine a world without us and wonder if our lives will be remembered, a concern no plant or animal has. So we build **memorials**.

This chapter is about Saraswati, knowledge, churned in imagination, a uniquely human currency. It is an essential ingredient of the 'business' body but the least understood. We focus on ideas and skills that make us smart. Education is now just vocational training. Myths are confused with history and reduced to tribal lore that serve politicians.

We are not encouraged to study our own minds, our own lives, our relationships, our yearning to be violent and competitive. Psychology is presented as something akin to pseudoscience, magical, otherworldly and spiritual, simply because we cannot measure it. And then we wonder why the richest and the most powerful amongst us are so depressed, angry and needy.

Step 1 of 3: Eat Better, to Nourish Your 'Business' Body

Business ▶ Knowledge ▶ **Ideas**

Plants and animals today live the same lives as they did a hundred, a thousand, ten thousand years ago. Humans, however, live very differently from their ancestors. We use different tools as compared to those who lived a thousand years ago. This is because humans have imagination with which they can conjure up alternate realities, which helps them come up with physical and mental tools to change the world around them.

Humans inherit knowledge from the past, refine it in the present and transmit it to the future. We are a learning species. That is why Saraswati is unique to humans. On our own, we observe, we infer, we compare. With others, we listen, discuss, debate. All this expands our mind with new ideas, new possibilities that can increase our chances of survival, our capacity, capability and productivity, improve our living conditions, fill our lives with greater pleasure and assurance.

We use mathematics to find the order in chaos. We use metaphors to communicate our feelings. Pattern-understanding improved exponentially with the development of better measuring tools and the evolution of mathematics. Technology became more predictable when we abandoned faith-based learning and embraced scepticism-based learning.

> **What new technology do you have today that did not exist ten years ago? What did your parents have that you do not?**

But as curiosity about the objective world has improved, curiosity about the subjective world has dropped. We have become so focused on the material and the universal that we have lost interest in symbols and metaphors, in art, stories, songs and music that once revealed the psychological, the cultural and the personal. In seeking one truth, we have lost sight of the infinite.

Step 1 of 3: Eat Better, to Nourish Your 'Business' Body

Business ▶ Knowledge ▶ **Curriculum**

Humans study nature, culture and the self. The study of nature involves the study of objects (physics) and organisms (biology) and their constituents (chemistry). Material science is objective, based solely on measurement and experimentation. It is sceptical of opinions, arguments and interpretations. It seeks objectivity established by verifiable proof.

The study of society involves figuring out the creation and distribution of wealth (economics) and power (politics) and about human organization in pre-industrial (anthropology) and post-industrial (sociology) societies. Social science is only partially objective, as we cannot experiment with humans, and rely on past data only. It involves logical interpretations and informed arguments. But these remain subjective and so can always be challenged.

The study of the self involves analysing how humans express emotions through stories (literature, fables, parables, legends), symbols (art, architecture) and rituals (music, dance, theatre, festivals, ceremonies, rites of passage). It is the world of metaphor, not logic or mathematics. It is totally outside the reach of science as it explores the non-measurable manifestations of hunger and fear. Humans have always relied on culturally transmitted stories, symbols and rituals to anchor their identity.

Modern society, however, dismissed cultural truths as false knowledge. Philosophers, spellbound by the scientific process, sought a singular truth based on logic. It ignored explorations of imagined hungers and imagined fears. Today, science can tell us that the human body needs carbohydrates, fats and proteins to survive. Science cannot explain the food takes in different kitchens. It cannot decide which is the most rational way to eat – with chopsticks, with cutlery, with our hands.

> What subject at school taught you how to cope with disappointment? Did you ever take your child to a museum to tell them about historical failures?

Any attempt to find a scientific and universal answer will lead to cultural wars. We can never know how the same food tastes on another's tongue, even if tools can index the sourness, sweetness and bitterness of various food items. The world thus does not reveal all its mysteries. Much knowledge bypasses the scientific process.

Step 1 of 3: Eat Better, to Nourish Your 'Business' Body

Business ▶ Knowledge ▶ **Transmission**

Plants and animals do not go to school. Their learning is intuitive, embedded in their biology. Humans need to be educated. We need to learn about nature, culture and the self. Traditionally, family transmitted vocational skills and social skills. In modern society, this is outsourced to schools and colleges and universities which teach state-approved curriculum. For understanding the self, we are on our own.

In the Ramayana, Ram gets theory education in Vasishta's school and practical education when Vishwamitra drags him to the forest. Ram does not choose his role in society. But Ram is a prince. When he is reborn as Krishna and raised by cowherds, he has no formal education. But when his aristocratic roots are revealed, he is tutored by Sandipani on the refined ways of conducting himself.

In a modern society, ideally everyone should get the same education, the same opportunity. But that means erasure of family and clan knowledge. Modern society outsources all learning to skill – either private or state-owned. These institutions teach all children universal survival and social skills and ignore cultural sensitivity. Higher education offers the option of vocational skills.

Those with money, influence or merit get into institutions that can afford the best teachers. Family education is now seen as optional, as students are being trained to serve as employees in corporations and industries that seek skill, not personality. In every school, teachers transmit information.

In the West, the burden of learning rests with teachers. In the East, the burden of learning rests with students. To transform information into knowledge, the receiver needs to consume it, digest and assimilate it. These are not in the transmitter's control. Drona taught archery to his son, Ashwatthama, but he was no match for the talented Arjuna.

Access to knowledge is theoretically open to all. But while denial of food amplifies hunger in all, denial of knowledge does not generate curiosity in everybody. As animals, food is our default need. Knowledge is new to the evolutionary process. It demands new neural networks. We would rather outsource it, like labour.

> Whose history does the school teach? Why not your family history?

Business ▶ Knowledge ▶ **Filter**

In the Mahabharata, Ekalavya and Karna wanted to be archers but Drona refused to train either one because they were not from royal families. Ekalavya observed Drona teaching his students and taught himself archery. Furious, Drona asked Ekalavya to cut his thumb off so he could never compete with Arjuna. Karna lied and learnt archery from Drona's teacher, Parashurama. When the lie was discovered, Parashurama cursed Karna that he would lose all memory of what he learnt at the moment he would need it the most.

Hoarding of knowledge gives communities a competitive advantage and this was fiercely protected. In India, preventing inter-caste marriage was a way of ensuring vocational knowledge systems stayed within the community. In a traditional society, questioning elders and teachers is frowned upon. This ensures traditional ideas are transmitted unchallenged which ensures social structures remain unchanged.

Internal knowledge is threatened by external knowledge. Monotheistic cultures survive by declaring all other faiths as heresies to be treated with ruthless violence. The church objected to the rise of science as the new knowledge created a new class of technocrats, entrepreneurs, industrialists and bankers who challenged their patrons, the landed aristocrats. To expand knowledge, one has to be sceptical and challenge what is inherited and be curious about other people's truth. But one does not have to reject old knowledge.

In the West, the Old Testament is discarded with the coming of the New Testament. Likewise, the rise of scientific knowledge meant the fall of religious knowledge. This led to expansion of material knowledge, and contraction of cultural or psychological knowledge. We now know a lot about distant stars and very less about human hungers and insecurities and how they give rise to different cultures. Cultural truths seek to regulate the human need for domination and territory, hence the borders and hierarchies reinforced by stories, symbols and rituals.

In trying to create an efficient society, science proposed standardization and one truth. Such ideas dissolve individual and cultural identity and are fiercely resisted. Today, attempts to impose a single value system around the world is fiercely resisted. Feminism, gay rights, queer rights, trans rights are being seen not as universal ideas but as Western ideas.

> Will you tell your children that your ancestors were killers, murderers and rapists? How do you know they were not?

We will understand other people's truths not by being combative but by being curious. People's truths do not carry the burden of evidence. They are indifferent to the judgement of others, howsoever scientific.

Step 1 of 3: Eat Better, to Nourish Your 'Business' Body

Business ▶ Knowledge ▶ **Memories**

The curious know that no one knows everything. That the more you know, the less you understand. We still do not know what happens after death. Why are we alive? Why can we imagine but not experience immortality? We comfort ourselves with rituals and beliefs and convince ourselves that life has a purpose and meaning other than eating and feeding. We cannot accept that despite the knowledge within us, and the wealth and power around us, our body is just food in the natural world.

We can give away our wealth and power before we die. We can transform some of our knowledge into information and transmit it using language. Balladeers and historians can tell our tales. Monuments may reveal our might. Museums can store our memories. But we cannot leave behind subjective experiences, the way we see, smell, hear, taste, touch and imagine the world. That is unique to us. It dies with us.

In the Ramayana, when Ravana is dying, he is asked by Ram if there is one lesson humans should remember. Ravana replies: We are naturally drawn to things that hurt us, never to things that help us. In the Mahabharata, the Yaksha asks Yudhishthira to tell him about the most wondrous thing on earth. Yudhishthira replies: Every day men die, the rest live as if they are immortal.

Escape the Bakasura Trap

We can leave behind material wealth and technology. We can leave behind skills and toolkits for survival. We can leave behind laws and structures that ensure there is order and justice, and repayment of debts. We can leave behind information, our anxieties and anger even, but not our experience or our wisdom. In the natural history of the world, we have been animals longer than we have been humans, and so tales of scarcity and terror seem more real than tales of abundance and affection. We have more memories of war, than peace. No parent can guarantee that their child will not go to the therapist to discuss childhood trauma.

> **What do you remember about your grandparents? What will you be remembered for? Are you sure?**

 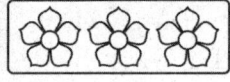 

Step 2 of 3: Kill Less, to Retrain Your 'Behavioural' Body

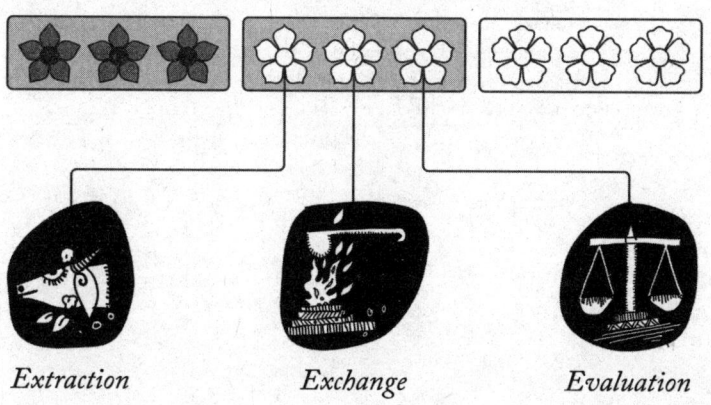

Extraction *Exchange* *Evaluation*

Behaviour body = The task of your life. What you do? To be efficient, effective or productive? To be stronger? Smarter? To win? To get revenge? To hack the system? Get the most for the least? Be bored? Be right? Be righteous? To not bother with measures or evaluations or balance sheets? Repay debts? Reclaim what is owed to you? To lend with expectations or invest without expectations? Invest in my people? Invest in neighbours? Invest in strangers?

Bhima kills a Kaurava

After his encounter with Hanuman, Bhima looked at the forest around him. This had been home when he was orphaned. This was his refuge when the Kauravas burnt his home. This was his shelter when the Pandavas were exiled. The forest had always welcomed the Pandavas, but the Pandavas had burnt the forest to the ground to build their city. He remembered the cries of the plants and animals that were burnt alive so that Indraprastha could rise in all its grandeur. That slaughter could have been avoided if the Kauravas had simply shared the family wealth. That could also have been avoided if the

Pandavas did not have the burning desire to build a city that would outshine the city of their cousins.

Bhima remembered the unprovoked attack on the kingdom of Panchala, that was conquered and split into two, much to the satisfaction of Drona, their teacher. The Panchala king had mocked Drona's poverty once and called him an inferior, unworthy of friendship. Now, they were equal.

Bhima remembered ripping the tyrant Jarasandha of Magadha into two so that the Pandavas could declare themselves sovereigns. How was Jarasandha, who extorted tribute from weaker kings, any different from Baka?

Bhima recalled the violence within families. The Pandavas were denied access to their inheritance by their own uncle and cousins. Kunti always favoured the eldest, Yudhishthira, and her youngest, Arjuna, at the cost of her middle child. Bhima recalled how his brother's authority over him prevented him from stopping the foolhardy gambling match.

In the gambling hall, Bhima witnessed the pretence of non-violence, how laws and agreements were manipulated to justify the public abuse of Draupadi. Her status of royalty had failed to protect her.

Step 2 of 3: Kill Less, to Retrain Your 'Behavioural' Body

Finally, he saw the fear in the eyes of the plants and animals he had crushed as he made his way to the flower that would make Draupadi happy. How was he different from Drona, Bakasura and Jarasandha? Given a chance, would he behave differently from Kunti, Yudhishthira, Dhritarashtra or the Kauravas?

Later, when the Pandavas hid as servants in the palace of Virata, in the final year of exile, Bhima saw first-hand the abuse endured by those who serve at the hands of those who are supposed to be caretakers of people.

Still later, in the war at Kurukshetra, Bhima killed all his cousins, enabling the Pandavas to reclaim the land the Kauravas had usurped. But victory came at a cost. The Pandavas lost all their children. They mourned as much as Dhritarashtra, father of the Kauravas. The old, blind king wanted to touch the arms of the man who killed all his sons. An iron statue in the likeness of Bhima was placed before him. Dhritarashtra hugged the statue with such force that the image was pulverized.

Bhima realized that his uncle saw him as the villain, and considered his own sons as victims, when they could have easily averted the war by accepting the terms of compromise. Furious, Bhima decided to teach the self-indulgent Dhritarashtra a lesson. In the days that followed, during every mealtime, Bhima

Escape the Bakasura Trap

would gleefully describe how he killed each of his cousins. The sound of their bones breaking, their entrails ripping, them screaming. This would hurt Dhritarashtra deeply; he would stop eating and start weeping. Unable to bear the repeated humiliation, Dhritarashtra eventually decided to leave the palace, preferring the terrors of the forest to the cruelty of Bhima. Once again, Bhima was seen as a villain, a tormentor of the old, blind, childless former king.

Overpowering his pompous friend was necessary for Drona's satisfaction. Killing Bakasura was necessary to protect the villagers. Burning the forest was necessary to build a home. Killing a tribute-seeking tyrant was necessary to establish sovereignty. Killing to reclaim one's own property was justified. Vengeance was justified. But was the resulting pain and suffering justified? Could rationalizing an action prevent the repercussions? For Dhritarashtra, his sons are victims, no matter what the Pandavas say. Is Dhritarashtra's rage justified as he mourns the loss of his children? Is Bhima's psychological abuse justified against an old, childless ex-king? Was Virata's ill-treatment of his servants justified? Lawyers can rationalize and tip any measuring scale in the client's favour. But who are they rationalizing to? Who decides the value of pain and the value of retribution? The more we rationalize violence and deny its inevitable consequences, the more fear we spread around us, the more predators, rivals and pretenders we create who bear a grudge against us. It

Step 2 of 3: Kill Less, to Retrain Your 'Behavioural' Body

is not a healthy ecosystem. We create a zone of fear, where everyone is on edge. Can non-violence be an option?

Bhima then became aware of his 'behavioural' body, his responses to the world that were so different from the responses of plants and animals. Plants and animals grab food. Humans can give food, to strangers even. And receive food from strangers. Plants and animals do not negotiate. They do not have the wherewithal to do so. Humans can. We can exchange, with anyone. We evaluate everything. We have measuring scales to judge the world around us. We seek control, certainty, predictability and profit. We can argue and justify anything. No plant or animal does that. The wild will not be domesticated. The domesticated will be exploited. This 'behavioural' body of humans is typically capable of three activities that the Rishis codified as sacred rituals:

A. **Extraction** was codified as the ritual of 'bali', where a goat would be beheaded or a coconut would be smashed in a single swift move and offered to the spirits of the forest.

B. **Exchange** was codified as the ritual of yagna to win favours from the gods (Devas) and ancestors (Pitr) who lived in the sky.

C. **Evaluation** was codified as the ritual of tula (pan balance), by which people could make gifts equal to their weight and value.

In this section, the second of the three steps, we will pay attention to our actions that shape the world around us.

Escape the Bakasura Trap

It will reveal the violence of the Bakasura Trap that we deny. Bakasura typically loves extraction. He even turns exchange into extraction, getting more by giving less, using talent and tricks to ensure he is always the winner. Thus, he accumulates more than Lakshmi and Durga, blissfully ignoring self-knowledge. Our 'behavioural' body reveals the kind of 'business' body we seek to wrap ourselves with.

Step 2 of 3: Kill Less, to Retrain Your 'Behavioural' Body

Behaviour ▶ **Extraction**

In nature, there is no concept of ownership. Plants grab sunlight and water without consent. Herbivores grab plant flesh without consent. Carnivores grab animals without consent. This is extraction. All consumption is violent. If we do not kill, we cannot eat or feed or be fed.

i. Culture engages in violence to extract **resources** from nature. Trees are cut for wood, rocks melted for metal, weeds uprooted to favour crops, animals gelded to make them docile.

ii. Humans resist domestication. They protest when forced to do **labour** for other people's leisure. Unless they get fair remuneration.

iii. Humans haggle over their fair **share.** Pecking orders in animals are meritocratic. But humans favour insiders and superiors.

iv. The strong use talent and the smart use tricks to corner the larger share. The hungry then turn into raiders and attack the hoarders. This is called **justice**.

v. Stories are used to **justify** extracting, the hoarding, the raiding. A good storyteller can make anything moral and ethical.

Escape the Bakasura Trap

This chapter is about extraction, the default programming of our 'behavioural' body. Since we are being conditioned to consume more, we extract more and so kill more. Wary of this, the ancients decided to sensitize humans about the cost of consumption by designing the ritual of bali, where goats are beheaded and coconuts smashed in the pursuit of food.

Step 2 of 3: Kill Less, to Retrain Your 'Behavioural' Body

Behaviour ▶ Extraction ▶ **Resources**

In the Vedas, there is the story of Bhrigu who witnesses the afterlife. He sees those who ate animals howl like animals as they are eaten by animals, mimicking the cry of creatures they butchered for their feasts. He also sees those who ate plants scream soundlessly as they are eaten by plants, as they never heard the screams of the cereals, pulses, legumes, roots, shoots and fruits they had plucked, deskinned, chopped, crushed, boiled and roasted in their kitchens. Thus, Vedic myth draws attention to how life feeds on life. In the industrial world, the pain of animals is ignored.

In the Vedic world, even plants felt pain, an idea that was erased in later times. To shun violence entirely, the Jain monk refuses to consume anything. He wears no clothes. He has no home. He wanders the earth, eating less and less until one day he starves to death, having fully conquered hunger and fear. This was the Jain path of the true conquerors, the Jinas, those who strive to overpower hunger and fear.

> How many trees were slaughtered to make the wooden furniture of your house? How many birds and insects on those trees lost their food for your home?

The idea of nature alive, of being a Goddess, is missing in monotheistic faiths. In Biblical myth, the god who creates nature gives it as dominion to man to consume. In Greek myth, nature is a chaotic force, a wild monster, full of wild nymphs and unrestrained satyrs, that humans need to tame. In Babylonian myth, nature was the wild Tiamat who had to be subjugated by the hero-god Marduk.

When nature is seen as non-living, then violence against nature is not disturbing. That is why industries do not think twice about polluting the air, the rivers, the soil and the sea, even though shareholders proclaim they are vegetarians, because they do not wish to hurt cattle, sheep, goats, pigs, chicken and fish.

Step 2 of 3: Kill Less, to Retrain Your 'Behavioural' Body

Behaviour ▶ Extraction ▶ **Labour**

There is no holiday in nature. Holidays are a human concept. In Biblical myth, God rests after creating the world on the seventh day. So humans also seek a holiday on the seventh day. No one can decide which day of the week it was: Muslims say Friday, Jews say Saturday, Christians say Sunday. To make peace, in America, Jewish labourers and Christian entrepreneurs came up with the concept of the weekend.

But there are no holidays for wives and mothers who do domestic chores, or for cooks and cleaners to whom this labour is outsourced. Humans seek holidays. We create a surplus, for days when we can consume without labouring, or to hire labour who can work while we relax. We get others to cook and clean, take care of our children, make our body beautiful, tend to our fields, keep watch over our flocks, fight our enemies and pay our bills. We extract labour from other humans just as we extract resources from nature.

As children, we are indulged by our parents, who feed us and clean us. Thus, every human, rich or poor, has a memory of paradise – a time when one lived in leisure without labour. In the old days, labour was obtained through slavery. Later, it involved paying fair wages. The servant was called a service-provider to raise the dignity of his job. Now, we seek machines, robots and artificial intelligence to replace people who demand more wages, and to do jobs that have been stripped of dignity.

Escape the Bakasura Trap

Children can today be borne by surrogate mothers, breast-fed by wetnurses, raised by nannies, tutored by teachers, trained by coaches, advised by counsellors. We have effectively found ways to outsource parenting. Financial instruments have been created so that money makes money in the stock market, and we can earn an income without actually doing any labour.

In Sumerian myth, the gods created humans to do labour so they could enjoy leisure. Sumerian kings are shown carrying bricks to build temples. In Biblical myth, humans have to do labour because they broke God's laws. Labour is repentance for sins. Many Jains, Buddhists and Hindus outsource tasks that involve violence, such as farming, in order to reduce their karmic debt. They do not see harnessing labour itself as violence.

> How many people are required to make your home comfortable? Have you forgotten the invisible folks who clean your sewage?

Step 2 of 3: Kill Less, to Retrain Your 'Behavioural' Body

Behaviour ▶ Extraction ▶ **Share**

After collaborating during a hunt, there is competition within the pack. The strong get more, the weak get less, the weakest take the leftovers. But who is strong among humans: the one with tools, the one with weapons, the one with ideas or the one with charm? What about the loyal and the rival? What about favourites?

A king was asked how a widow should share a pot of rice with her three children: one child is strong and needs more food to do labour; one child is sick and needs more food to heal; one child is smart and needs more food to learn. Is there a right way to divide the pot of rice so everyone feels happy and everyone gets what they want? The king cannot answer. The mother cannot decide as she is torn between logic and love. Children who get the larger share are always seen as the favourites. The one who gets to eat first is the most loved. The least loved gets the leftovers. In feudal societies, the insiders eat first, and amongst insiders the superiors eat first.

Those who are valued more tend to get the larger share – but they use that large share to ensure they keep getting the large share. Thus, the first generation of success is based on meritocracy. But the second generation is usually based on nepotism. The first time, you win like a Greek hero on individual action. The second time, your children benefit on account of being the Chosen People favoured by God.

Escape the Bakasura Trap

We extract for insiders. And among insiders we prefer family. And within family we prefer the elders, the loyal and the lovable. There are no global standard rules of distribution; it is always cultural. Traditional societies favoured elders. The young had to be content with the leftovers. Socialists speak of inclusion, equality and equity. Everyone must eat together. No one gets first right to feed. No one gets special treatment. But then no one feels special. No one feels motivated to work harder, be better. The strong resent the weak. The smart resent the simple.

Borders and hierarchies and the share of food tell us who we are, where we belong, who is above us, who is below us, who feeds us, who we are supposed to feed, and who we are exposed to eat. Distribution is so difficult that in Hindu mythology, God is referred to as Ishwar (the only one who has right over everything) and Bhagavan (the only one who knows how to apportion correctly).

> Should the smart daughter get more money or the disabled son? Did the gender or the adjective bother you more?

Step 2 of 3: Kill Less, to Retrain Your 'Behavioural' Body

Behaviour ▶ Extraction ▶ **Justice**

The earliest kings controlled water bodies and canal irrigation. Only those who obeyed were given access to water, hence they could grow food. Control over food gave birth to power. Hoarders had more power over people. Surplus food funded philosophers, singers, musicians, dancers, entertainers, architects, mathematicians, artists, those who were not directly involved in food production.

Those who had no lands to till and labour to give starved. They turned tools into weapons and became raiders, threatening hoarders. Later, they took control of the land and the labour. Those with weapons were the first thieves, the first enslavers. Weapon-users became heroes when they fought rival raiders and defended the food-hoarders. They charged tax for their services.

Weapons thus controlled wealth, wealth controlled people. But there was intense competition. So creative folks were sought out: those who could invent better tools and better weapons, so better ways of raiding and hoarding and controlling and taxing could be devised. These were the smart folks: the logicians, the magicians, the scientists, the inventors and innovators, the idea-generators. There were rivals here too, as there were rivals amongst food-hoarders and weapon-users.

Escape the Bakasura Trap

> Will you pay more to your loyal staff or your disloyal son? What if you find your loyal staff making fun of you behind your back?

The food-hoarder, the weapon-user and the knowledge-maker, masters of Lakshmi, Durga and Saraswati, became the first elites. Capitalism called them successful. Socialism called them oppressors. Libertarianism refused to judge them and encouraged everyone to be one of them.

Step 2 of 3: Kill Less, to Retrain Your 'Behavioural' Body

Behaviour ▶ Extraction ▶ **Justification**

Those with knowledge realized that language was also a tool to control humans. Language enables us to communicate technical knowledge. Language also helps us control people. Words can be violent: They can inflict hurt that is never seen. Words can energize us, make us feel powerful and desirable. Instead of whips and sticks and stones, or with promises of food and leisure, people could be made to obey by praising them or insulting them. Words can be used to convince people, sow doubt, establish laws and invent stories.

Stories are of different kinds. Stories to entertain. Stories to explain. Stories to remember. Stories to warn. Stories to give hope. Stories of origins. Stories to convince. Stories to justify.

Stories told us what was right and wrong, good and bad, what were the causes of events and the consequences of actions. Stories gave identity, justified hoarding and raiding, fuelled revolutions. Stories for capitalists justified hoarding and vilified raiders. Stories of socialists vilified hoarders and justified raiding. Stories of libertarians justified individual choice. Stories convinced humans to respect the law and voluntarily domesticate themselves. Stories create the three worlds: Those above are either gods or oppressors and those below are either demons or the oppressed. Stories explain the human condition, mobilize labour, justify leisure, restrain greed, question exploitation, grant dignity, by establishing concepts like justice, equality, God, heaven, hell and rebirth, which do not exist in nature.

> How many people see you as the villain of their story? How many people do you see as the villain of your story?

But stories only work if they are trusted. A new storyteller could argue that the old storyteller was brainwashing them. The idea of one true god, sold by missionaries, failed to unite the world. Nor did the story that there is no god. A world without stories is a world without meaning. We become animals, hungry and frightened, with no identity, and so easy to dehumanize.

Step 2 of 3: Kill Less, to Retrain Your 'Behavioural' Body

Behaviour ▶ Exchange

In nature, we do see exchange alongside extraction. Plants produce flowers and fruits, offering nectar and flesh to bees, birds and beasts, who help plants pollinate and spread their seed in exchange. Herbivores produce surplus babies to feed carnivores so that those who survive can reproduce. Carnivores, by killing herbivores, ensure they do not overgraze. Thus, through exchange, the plant kingdom helps herbivores, herbivores help carnivores, and carnivores help the plant kingdom.

i. Humans can choose to trade over raiding and hoarding. We can **receive** rather than grab. This allows for cooperation and collaboration. We exchange not just Lakshmi, but also Durga and Saraswati.

ii. Exchange creates an ecosystem of debit and credit. Everyone has a balance sheet of loans to repay and reclaim. Debts create **obligations**.

iii. Those who invest regularly and those who repay on schedule are most **popular**.

iv. The professional only focuses on what is given and received, and how it is given and received, the 'business' body and 'behavioural' body. These are transactions. Here, everyone is focused on their own hunger. It establishes **networks**.

v. To build **relationships,** we have to expand our gaze, look beyond what people have and what people do at who people are.

This chapter is about yagna, exchange, where you extract for the other and the other extracts for you. The debit of killing is balanced by the credit of feeding. It draws our attention to the hunger of the other. It is the cornerstone of the Bhima Escape.

Step 2 of 3: Kill Less, to Retrain Your 'Behavioural' Body

Behaviour ▶ Exchange ▶ **Receive**

Plants grab. Animals grab. Humans can receive and give. The serving spoon on the dining table is a reminder of the human ability to serve others. While birds do feed their young, there is never any reciprocation.

Long ago, the creator-god Brahma invited his children for a meal. When the food was served, he asked his children to eat but without bending their elbow. This was impossible, said some children, who turned into stones that never eat. Those who bent their heads and licked the plate turned into plants and animals that always grow and move towards food. But some children picked up food and fed those in front of them. They were humans. They hoped that those fed would reciprocate. Some did, some did not. Those who did repaid their debt. Those who did not remained in debt. To reduce debt, humans reciprocate. The Vedic ritual of yagna thus came into being.

In yagna, you give what you have to get what you want. The one who gives first is the Yajamana. The one who receives first is the Devata. The Yajamana takes risks as there is no guarantee of return. The Devata takes no risk but bears the burden of debt until he reciprocates. The Yajamana said, 'Svaha!' which means, 'This what was mine is now yours.' He hoped the Devata would say, 'Tathastu!' which means, 'May your desires manifest.'

Escape the Bakasura Trap

> **What did you give to your parents to get your inheritance? What did your children give you in order to get your inheritance?**

In Vedic times, it was an exchange of intangible things between humans and gods: praise given to acknowledge invisible gods and grace manifested proving their existence. In later temple traditions, the exchange was more tangible. The deity in the temple was given food (naivedya) and blessings took the form of food (prasad). The yagna is not a contract: there is no give and take; you give to receive. It's voluntary. There is no guarantee of return.

Step 2 of 3: Kill Less, to Retrain Your 'Behavioural' Body

Behaviour ▶ Exchange ▶ **Obligation**

In a yagna, you give for two reasons. You are repaying a debt. Or you are creating credit, investing for a future return. You receive for two reasons. You are taking a loan. Or you are reclaiming what is owed to you. Yagna thus creates a balance sheet. Debt if you take. Credit if you give. Debt gives immediate joy and pain later. Credit gives immediate pain but future joy.

Reclaiming loans and giving credit created the ladder. Taking loans was the snake in the game of snakes-and-ladders invented by Indian merchants. Not surprisingly, historians say India was the land of double-income bookkeeping. Those with credit are born into privilege, as per this belief. Those in debt are born in hell, burdened by obligation. Freedom is being free of debit and credit, pain and pleasure. This way of thinking was unique to India.

Across the Arabian Sea, a different model was followed. One based on obedience, justice and gratitude. Young men of Arabia followed old tribal leaders on raids. The leader offered the promise of paradise or Jannat to those who followed him and threatened hell or Jahannam to those who disobeyed. A good leader kept his word and was venerated by all. With excess loot, bad leaders bought slaves. These slaves offered undying loyalty to the master in exchange for the good life. As directed by the master, they participated in raids. But they had no claim on the loot. They were eternally grateful for whatever the Sultan gave them. This allowed bad leaders to accumulate more wealth, more slaves, and engage in more raids. When Islam arose, slavery was banned. Sharing equally was considered justice, the sign of good leadership.

In Arabian myth, when Adam and Eve were cast out of Eden, Eve fell in Arabia, but Adam fell in India. The two were connected by the monsoon winds, a memory of ancient sea trade. Arabs took the Indian system of the balance sheet, of debit and credit, of the double-entry book system, and taught it to the children of Eve. But the double-entry system worked only in cultures that believe in many lives, where balance sheets explained the inequality at the time of birth. In cultures that believe in one life, inequality in society was the result of unfair distribution of common wealth by bad leaders.

> How many people contributed to your success? How many people owe their success?

Step 2 of 3: Kill Less, to Retrain Your 'Behavioural' Body

Behaviour ▶ Exchange ▶ **Popularity**

If the Devata gives what the Yajamana wants, he is likely to be invited again for another exchange. This is called 'repeat order' in business. If the Devata keeps giving what the Yajamana wants, the Yajamana is likely to refer the Devata to others. This is called 'referral'. Repeat orders and referrals are indicators of a Devata's demand, and the key to sustainable prosperity.

Bakasura is shunned as he only takes and does not give. Bhima is sought as he offers the promise of security and delivers again and again. The Devata who delivers customer delight is sought by all. The Devata also rushes to the Yajamana who customizes his offering to what the Devata wants. We love people who treat us as special. The privileged customer, the one who is loyal, the one who is reliable, the one who gives more, the one who is always prompt, is always special and in demand.

If the Yajamana does not want to share the Devata with others, he keeps the Devata secret and exclusive. Monogamy is such an exchange, where the husband and wife keep their services exclusive to each other, as in the case of Ram and Sita in the epic Ramayana. Shurpanakha wants what Ram has; her brother, Ravana, wants what Sita has. Neither cares for consent. They are not invited to the exchange, so they raid and try to take what they want by force. In the Ramayana, those who raid rather than trade are Rakshasa, to be killed.

In the Mahabharata, when a man marries many women, as in the case of Arjuna in the Mahabharata, he becomes the Yajamana. There is competition between the Devata-wives, who wonder which wife he will invite to the exchange. When a woman marries many men, as in the case of Draupadi, she is not allowed to be the Yajamana who invites any Devata as per her wish. Rules are made to prevent rivalry between the husbands: Each one will have sequential access to her, one year at a time. We can say the Devata-husbands create a cartel to control the polyandrous Yajamana. But while they can measure the time spent with the wife, they cannot measure the quality of affection she showers on them individually.

In polytheism, every god has something to offer. So no one is all-powerful. So every god has to be wooed. There is constant negotiation. It's a dynamic ecosystem where the giver and the receiver, the Yajamana and the Devata, are gods, as both have something the other wants. However, in monotheism, there is one god, the source of all wealth. Here, there is no room for negotiation. The deity gives, the devotee receives. The deity only seeks obedience and submission, the erring devotee seeks mercy. This model is popular in feudal systems, where the king has control over all wealth and power. This model is replicated in monopolies, in societies where the state has all the power, and everyone has to obey and align.

Step 2 of 3: Kill Less, to Retrain Your 'Behavioural' Body

In the Ramayana, Ravana wants to be all-powerful and demands loyalty. Ram is not all-powerful. He helps Sugriva defeat Vali and become king of Kishkindha. Sugriva repays his debt by helping Ram rescue Sita from the clutches of Ravana. There is interdependence. That is yagna.

> Do you seek out your customers or do they seek you out?

Behaviour ▶ Exchange ▶ **Network**

In tribal societies, everyone does everything. Everyone knows how to make pots, weave cloth and find food. There is no need for outsiders, provided there is enough food. But when there is scarcity of food and resources, tribes need to raid or trade. Raiding creates war. Trading creates a market. A market creates a network. Such networks transform a culture into a civilization.

It all began when labour was divided. Women stayed by the fire to take care of children and focused on sedentary tasks like cooking and weaving. Men ventured beyond the fire into the dark wilderness, took risks to find new sources of food. Men got access to more women by finding better food and providing more security. Women got access to more men by providing better hospitality services. Men who liked leisure enjoyed women who could labour. Women who enjoyed leisure enjoyed men who could labour. Those too old to fend for themselves exchanged their knowledge and skills and stories for care.

Gradually, communities focused on specialized tasks: farming, herding, hunting, fishing, weaving, pottery, carpentry, mining, transporting, accounting, entertaining. This was possible when other communities agreed to become specialized, too, focusing on providing goods and services that others needed. Potter communities depended

Step 2 of 3: Kill Less, to Retrain Your 'Behavioural' Body

on farmers to grow food and weavers to make cloth. Barbers thrived because potters and farmers and weavers needed their services.

Markets emerged where the hungry (needy, lazy, bored) were buyers and those with food (goods, services, ideas) were sellers. That the market provided a variety of novel and rare goods revealed the widening of human hunger.

Markets encouraged comparison, jealousy, competition. Innovation threatened tradition. Those threatened built borders and walls. Those curious insisted on gateways, with gatekeepers, to filter in the good and filter out the bad. But there were always frightened hoarders who wanted to keep more and give less. There were also suspicious traders, eager to take more than give. Those who did not repay loans were not welcome to the market. Those who gave assurance of returns were always welcomed.

> **Do you have friends who hate paying staff on time? Do you pay your staff on time?**

Behaviour ▶ Exchange ▶ **Relationships**

A transaction is an exchange where we focus on what is being exchanged and how the exchange is being conducted. A relationship is an exchange where we also look at who is participating in the exchange. Modern impersonal business institutions strive to be the former. A yagna is about the latter. For the purpose of a yagna is to use the 'behavioural' body not just to influence the 'business' body but also the 'belief' body.

Once, there were two childhood friends who promised to share their fortunes with each other. Time treated them differently. One became rich. The other became poor. Desperate, the poor friend went to the rich friend hoping to get some help. In the Mahabharata, the poor friend was Drona. He reminded the rich friend, Drupada, king of Panchala, of the old promise. Drupada was offended by this tone of familiarity. He said friendship exists between equals. The poor can beg for help, like outsiders, not assume they are still insiders. A humiliated Drona walked away determined to teach arrogant Drupada a lesson. Years later, Drona's students raided Panchala and gave half of Drupada's kingdom to their teacher. Drona hugged a humbled Drupada as an equal, but now it was Drupada's turn to be angry and plot revenge. The spiral of vendetta culminated in the battle of Kurukshetra.

Step 2 of 3: Kill Less, to Retrain Your 'Behavioural' Body

In the Bhagavata, the same story has a twist. The poor friend, Sudama, does not eat for three days and offers the food to his rich friend, Krishna. Krishna accepts the gift gracefully and repays the debt with disproportionate generosity.

> Do you judge friends who yell at their incompetent staff? Do you see the incompetence of your staff or their powerlessness?

The Drona–Drupada story ends in a violent raid as Drupada refuses to give Drona the dignity of an insider and treats his request as extraction. The Sudama–Krishna story ends with joyful trade as Sudama does begin by asking, but also by giving. He becomes the Yajamana who invokes the Devata and the Devata reciprocates with empathy and grace. In either case, the exchange was not so much about the transfer of wealth, it was also about the yearning for human dignity and the search for kindness in the world.

Behaviour ▶ Evaluation

Plants and animals cannot measure. They do not strive for more, or to be better. They know their place in the food chain and the pecking order. Humans do not. We need to know our worth. A pan balance (tula) was used in Indian temple ceremonies to demonstrate our worth to the world. Everyone was expected to give something equal to their weight to the deity in the temple. The weight was objective. But the value of goods given was subjective.

i. We feel safe when expectations are set about what will be received in exchange for what is given. We call this **agreement**.

ii. We feel special when we are fed what we want, and given what everyone can eat. We call this **customization**.

iii. We can feel triumphant when we are able to trick others into giving more and accepting less. We call this **gamification**.

iv. We value leisure over labour so much that we are happiest when we get something for nothing. We call this **luck**.

v. We use stories to increase the value of goods and services of the same measure. We call it **branding**.

This chapter is about how we use measuring scales to define our worth. Hoarding starts being seen as a marker of success, not debt. This is what the Rishis called maya, or delusion.

Step 2 of 3: Kill Less, to Retrain Your 'Behavioural' Body

Behaviour ▶ Evaluation ▶ **Agreement**

Exchange can be annoying. What we receive may not match up to our expectations. Uttanaka spent years praising the gods in the hope they would give him a drop of the nectar of immortality. They did, but it was offered in an 'impure' bowl, made of a human skull, much to Uttanaka's disgust. The gods had given him what he wanted, but not in the way he wanted it. He felt cheated.

In the Gita, Krishna says that the Yajamana can control the input (bija, the seed), not the output (phala, the fruit). But humans want to control the output. So we created contracts with clear expectations from both parties. At work, the employer agrees to pay wages, and the employee agrees to gives services. Here, there is no receiving, only taking. The employer takes services; the employee takes wages. Failure to give leads to tension, fights and violence. The employer always feels the services rendered are not satisfactory. The employee always feels the remuneration is not adequate, as there are more and more expectations, higher and higher targets. Tracking systems can only measure targets and tasks. Not respect. Respect shown through protocols are ceremonial performances, not authentic. Both parties feel the noose around the neck. The lack of freedom.

Those who work more despite being paid less are seen as loyal employees; they are venerated and glamorized. The loyal do not have to be as effective as the professional as their employment is assured. Professionals cannot be trusted. They are like nymphs, those who go to the highest bidder and escape when they get the chance.

When asked which of his two sons should be given a wife, Shiva said it would be the one who goes around the world three times. Kartikeya, the mighty, ran around the oceans and the continents and the stars. Ganesha, the smart one, ran around his parents, and declared himself as the winner. He argued he went around his subjective world. Kartikeya was going around the objective world. Shiva had not specified which world they had to go around as both coexist and both matter equally. The objective world of matter and measurement. The subjective world of mind and values.

Those who value the material are unable to appreciate the cost of aesthetics, which is highly subjective. Those who value the measurable are unable to appreciate the cost of design, which is highly cultural. The scientist seeks the efficient, the effective, the productive, the ergonomic. None of these may add up to create something beautiful. Hence, we need contracts to set our expectations.

> How do you measure respect in a relationship? Have you met people who love insulting the receiver when paying what is due?

Step 2 of 3: Kill Less, to Retrain Your 'Behavioural' Body

Behaviour ▶ Evaluation ▶ **Customization**

In nature, there is diversity and meritocracy, but no equality. Every organism has its own context and has to fend for itself. No one is going to take care of them. However, in a nation-state, laws are supposed to treat all citizens equally. The murderer is a murderer, a rapist is a rapist. Their status in society makes no difference. At least in theory. But the rich murderer and the rich rapist can hire better lawyers and spin the case in their favour.

In many traditional societies, there were different laws for different groups of people. Modernity frowned upon such traditional society. Equality was held up as an ideal. But equality ends up being the opposite of diversity. This is because equality strives for homogeneity, giving the same opportunities to all. Diversity is heterogenous, different people have different needs and different opportunities. Heterogeneity leads to differentiation and discrimination. This results in hierarchy. With hierarchy comes inequality. In inequality there are oppressors and the oppressed. Justice is fighting oppressors, reducing inequality, moving towards less heterogeneity and more homogeneity. But humans do not like homogeneity or equality. We want to feel special, be different. Groups compete; we want to belong to special groups. Within groups, we want to stand out, be unique.

As per science, all humans are supposed to eat carbohydrates, fats and proteins. But everyone likes to eat them differently.

There are different cuisines in different cultures, each providing the same nutrition, but with different tastes and textures, some eaten with chopsticks, some eaten with cutlery and some with fingers. No cuisine is better or worse. Attempts to create a standard meal is met with resistance.

Yet, diversity is inefficient. It is easier for a canteen to serve the same food to all students the same way, every day. So capitalists prefer standardization – the dream of socialists. But every capitalist wants something unique served to him. For he wants to be special. Likewise, every socialist will argue differently to establish individuality.

> Did your parents see you or your report card? Do you see your child or their success?

Step 2 of 3: Kill Less, to Retrain Your 'Behavioural' Body

Behaviour ▶ Evaluation ▶ **Gamification**

When Narada was born, he wondered what the point of living was. He noticed everyone around him was running. They were busy in a race: outrunning the predator or the prey or the rival, forming allies to win. Even plants were competing with each other, for more sunlight, more water. The sense of triumph gave them purpose, filled them with exhilaration and made them feel heroic. Those who lost saw themselves as martyrs. He realized life was a game (leela) and it could be gamified by comparison and shifting the measuring scales.

And so Narada went around the world informing them about others who had better homes, better wives, more wealth, more power, more estates, more knowledge, more fans, more followers, more lovers. This made people anxious, angry, jealous. He realized everyone wanted to be glamorous, be envied by others, have more than others, be better than others. Competition made love purposeful. Triumphs made life delightful.

In the Ramayana, Ravana refuses to offer Hanuman a place to sit in his hall. So Hanuman extends his tail and coils it to make a seat for himself. The seat he creates is taller than Ravana's throne. Ravana feels so small that he decides to burn Hanuman's tail.

Escape the Bakasura Trap

In the Mahabharata, Ekalavya is so skilled an archer that he is able to silence a dog without killing it by shooting arrows into its mouth. Arjuna feels insecure. To ensure Arjuna remains the greatest archer in the world, Ekalavya is tricked into cutting his thumb which stabilizes his bow. Karna also turns out to be a better archer than Arjuna. So Arjuna refers to him as a charioteer's son, insulting his birth status constantly. Objective skills can be changed but subjective status cannot.

During the war, Arjuna's arrow pushes Karna's chariot a thousand feet behind. Karna's arrow pushes Arjuna's chariot only ten feet behind. When Krishna praises Karna instead of Arjuna, Arjuna asks for an explanation. Krishna explains that Karna's chariot has just two men on it. But Arjuna's chariot has one man and two gods: Krishna, who is Vishnu, as charioteer, and Hanuman on the flag above. So Karna's subjective output is many times greater than Arjuna's objective output. Scores do not tell the whole truth. The context of the score determines who is the real champion.

> Who is luckier: The one raised in an orphanage, one raised by parents, one raised by nannies?
> Who is luckier: The one born to rich parents or born to understanding parents?

Step 2 of 3: Kill Less, to Retrain Your 'Behavioural' Body

Behaviour ▶ Evaluation ▶ **Luck**

In an exchange, what we give is the denominator and what we get is the numerator. In an ideal world, the numerator should be always equal to the denominator. We should get what we give. But in the real world, some get multiples of what they give. And some get fractions of what they give. If you get more than you give, you are celebrated. If you get less than you give, you are pitied. If you get something without giving anything, you are called lucky. If you get nothing and lose everything, you are called unlucky.

Children who are born into rich families or to loving parents are considered lucky as they get everything by doing nothing. Buddhist myth explains such luck by viewing it as a return on investments made in previous lives. To increase future returns, one is encouraged to feed monks and spread the word of the Buddha. In the Buddhist world, there is a rush to feed senior monks, who are seen as giving better returns on investment.

Islamic myth accepts the luck of being born into a good family and to good parents as the will of God, for which one needs to be grateful. There is no previous life for investments or future life for returns. How one lives the privileged life is the investment, the returns of which manifest on Judgement Day. For in Islamic lore, the ones with more who give less are cast into hell (Jahannam) for disobeying God's law, while those with less who give more are taken to heaven

(Jannat) for obeying God's law. Rather than striving to be generous, lawyers in the Islamic world spin the law in their client's favour, or worse, their favour, while declaring God is merciful, forgiving those who hack the system.

Capitalism is about increasing our luck, finding strategies to get more and give less. To give the illusion of higher returns, for less effort, shopping malls give discounts and deals. Media houses refuse to pay young entertainers for their art and craft, insisting that the value of the exposure is much greater.

Socialism is about caring for the unlucky, creating laws to compel the lucky to give more to the unlucky. But humans find novel ways to give only that much of the measurable as is agreed upon and as little of the non-measurable. The employer gives fair wages on time as demanded by the contract (measurable currency) but is stingy with appreciation and respect (non-measurable currency). The employee does the job on time as instructed (measurable and agreed upon currency), but without passion, interest or excitement (non-measurable currency). There is no villain or victim here. Just humans who envy the lucky, and strive to be less unlucky.

> Do you prefer being called by your name or by passport number? Do you refer to the waiter or driver by name or job description?

Step 2 of 3: Kill Less, to Retrain Your 'Behavioural' Body

Behaviour ▶ Evaluation ▶ **Branding**

The price of luxury goods is far more than the cost of their manufacture. That is because the item is imprinted with a story. That story makes the item priceless. The buyer pays for the story, not the product.

A senior Jain monk once entered a market. The merchants there, who had never fed a single hungry beggar in their life, argued over who should have the honour to feed the monk. For the merchants, feeding a hungry man was of less value than feeding a monk, because the monk came imprinted with a story, the promise of spiritual merit. That imprinted story is what turns a commodity into a brand. It gives status to the owner. By buying and displaying an expensive brand, the owner declares his wealth to the world.

By securing a rare jewel, an antique, the owner demonstrates his power to the world. By getting Tansen to sing for him, Akbar told the whole world not just about his wealth and power, but also about his refined cultural tastes, his deep understanding of the classical arts. But Akbar could not get Baiju Bawra to sing for him. An eccentric musical genius, Baiju Bawra refused to be bought. By making himself inaccessible, choosing his own audience, his own song, in his own time, he made himself mysterious, mystical and invaluable. An annoyed Akbar got his royal bards to spread stories to tarnish Baiju's reputation as a snob who valued

Escape the Bakasura Trap

art more than people, lacking Tansen's humility. The value of Tansen's music and Baiju's music was shaped as much by the stories imprinted on them as by the experience of the listener.

Krishna was placed on a pan balance and weighed against what his queens valued the most. Krishna remained heavier than all of Satyabhama's jewels but lighter than Rukmini's tulsi sprig, imprinted with her love for Krishna. The story gave dignity to Krishna's poor devotees who saw how temple priests fawned over rich devotees.

A tribal youth always offered his hunt to Shiva, while a temple priest gives flowers. Shiva preferred the tribal offering as it was an expression of love while the priest was simply following a process, doing his duty. There was no love. The temple authorities saw meat as impure and the hunter as impure, and forbade the tribal from entering the temple. The story is told to remind everyone that the measuring scales of society need not align with the measuring scales of the gods. We choose the stories that devalue others and make us feel significant.

> Do you feel special when rules are broken just for you?
> Do you make people feel special by breaking rules for them?

Step 3 of 3: Feed More, to Sensitize Your 'Belief' Body

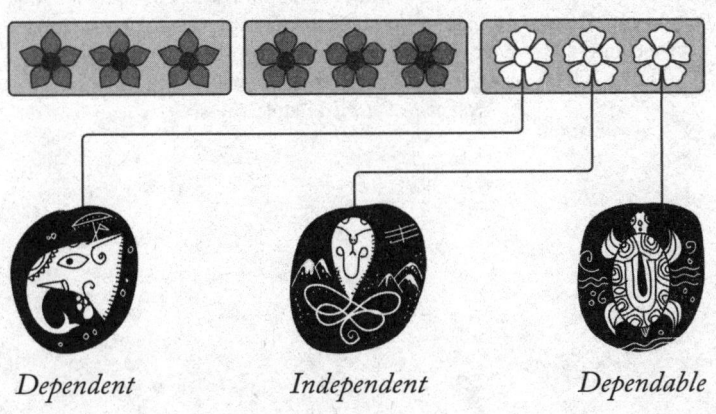

Dependent *Independent* *Dependable*

Belief body = The trackers of your life. What do you track? Who do you track? Do you give more or get more? Do you eat or feed? Do you judge or account? Do you smile at the competitive to make them feel good? Do you let people grow or do you control/enable their growth? Are you at peace with helplessness?

Bhima feeds Draupadi

When he returned with the golden flower, Bhima found Draupadi smiling. It was not the flower that made her smile; it was a magical vessel given to her by the gods. She was unhappy not because she was experiencing scarcity in the forest. She was unhappy because she could not feed everyone who paid her a visit there. Feeling sorry for her, the gods gave a magical vessel that would always be full of food until she ate from it. Then it would become empty, and resume producing food only the next day. Draupadi was happy eating only once a day, at the end of the day, because she finally had the means even in the forest to feed everyone who came to her home, even guests and strangers. Bhima watched as his dear wife starved the whole day to feed others. Draupadi's vessel could satisfy Bhima's endless hunger. However, if he did not rein in his hunger, Draupadi would never be able to eat a single meal. His food came at a cost – her starvation. Compassion for his dear wife helped him to outgrow his addiction to hunger and reduce the consequent violence.

As he restrained his hunger, his attention shifted from feeding himself to feeding others. He remembered wives who fed him, wives who he barely remembered. There was Hidimbi, that sister of Baka, who served his mother, his brothers and him, but whom he abandoned, on Kunti's orders, for better prospects. Even earlier, there was a nameless Naga woman who had rescued him and nursed him back to health when the Kauravas had attempted to drown him. Bhima realized he had never fed either wife. They never asked him to repay what he owed them. He thus became aware of how entitled a life he had lived.

Bhima thought of the times when he shook trees in the royal orchard until they yielded their fruits. He was too hungry to notice his hungry cousins who were climbing those very same trees for the very same fruits. The cousins fell with the fruits. This made Bhima laugh. He ate the fruits, ignoring the rising rage and resentment of his cousins. They never saw him as family, therefore. Just an intruder, an outsider, a rival, a threat.

Bhima's insight into hunger expanded in the final year of his exile, when the Pandavas had to live in hiding.

Step 3 of 3: Feed More, to Sensitize Your 'Belief' Body

If discovered by their cousins, they would have to repeat the forest exile. Bhima had to take a role that no one would imagine him capable of doing. He became a cook in a royal kitchen. As a result, he had to serve food to everyone in the household before he could eat. Here he got exposed to the hunger of strangers, the hunger of the privileged masters of the household, the hunger of the servants, the hierarchies within family and household revealed in who was fed when and how and what, everyone's unreasonable demands of the kitchen, and the cost of consumption: the groceries that had to be fetched, the utensils that had to be washed, the waste that had to be thrown, the complaints that had to be tolerated. Bhima, who was always fed more and fed first, learnt to see the hunger of those who ate least and ate last.

When it was clear that the Kauravas would not return Pandava lands, when war seemed increasingly inevitable, both the Pandavas and the Kauravas sought the help of the Yadava brothers, Krishna and Balarama. Kauravas took Krishna's army, Krishna became Arjuna's charioteer. Both Bhima and Duryodhana went to Balarama. Balarama had taught both of them mace warfare. Balarama, however, refused to participate in the war. He saw violence between family members as unethical and immoral, and impossible to justify. He went on a pilgrimage when the war began. When he returned, he was furious to learn that Bhima had broken the rules of duel and killed Duryodhana. On Krishna's advice, with a swing of his mace, Bhima had struck Duryodhana below the navel and broken Duryodhana's thigh. Krishna defended Bhima and argued that Balarama was ignoring the fact that Duryodhana was a king, who is supposed to be at least generous, if not fair. The generous help for no reason. The fair help because there is a reason. Duryodhana was rich enough to give a portion of his wealth to the Pandavas for the sake of peace. Instead, he used rules to justify denying them even a needlepoint of territory. His arguments were rooted in jealousy and spite. Why did Balarama not see that? Why did Balarama tolerate the legal sophistry? Why was he being so gullible and indulgent of Duryodhana? Why was generosity not being demanded of a king? If kings behaved like animals, focused on eating rather than feeding, were territorial and dominating, then why could they not be hunted like animals, using tricks and traps?

Repeated sojourns to the forest had made Bhima realize the difference between animals and humans. Animals eat and get eaten. Humans can feed and get fed. However, the entitled are fed but do not feed. The exploited feed and are not fed. Yudhishthira was so obsessed with his newfound power and the idea of winning that during that game of dice, despite the protests of his brothers, he kept on playing despite mounting losses. Duryodhana hated the Pandavas so much that he used all rules to justify not sharing anything

Step 3 of 3: Feed More, to Sensitize Your 'Belief' Body

with them. Balarama was so obsessed with appearances, social rules and the masquerade of peace that he failed to see why rules exist in the first place, and how the point of life is not to perform but to bring value to those around us. In the obsession with what we are hungry for, we do not see the killing that manufactures food, or the hunger and anger of those who are denied food. How we see the world, what we choose to see or not see, is a function of our imagined hungers and our imagined fears and our imagined confidence. Our lack of curiosity reveals who we are.

Thus, Bhima finally discovered the 'belief' body, wrapped deep within his 'behavioural' body, obscured by the dazzle of the 'business' body. Rishis referred to this body as 'dehi', the resident of the flesh (deha). The is the residence of our hungers, our fears, our ignorance. It influences what we see and how we see people around us.

A. We can stay **dependent** on food and treat everyone either as threat or opportunity, like Brahma, creator of the war zone.

B. We can become **independent** of food and indifferent to the hungry and the frightened, like Shiva, destroyer of the war zone.

C. We can be **dependable,** like Vishnu, feed the hungry, comfort the frightened and be resilient enough to make people responsible and accountable, thus transforming the war zone (Rana-Bhoomi) into the delight zone (Ranga-Bhoomi).

Escape the Bakasura Trap

In this section, the final step of our three-step process, we will do 'darshan' – see like the Rishis do. By being curious about what people seek and shun, we gain insight into their hungers and fears, which will reflect our own hunger and our fear. We then have the option to let the knowledge dilute our hunger and fear. The resulting contentment has the power to establish mangal (a finite ecosystem of pleasure) around us in the jungle (an infinite web of hunger and fear).

Step 3 of 3: Feed More, to Sensitize Your 'Belief' Body

Belief ▶ **Dependent**

Brahma is the creator in Hindu mythology. Not the creator of nature (as in Biblical myth), but the creator of his own world. Hindu myth values subjectivity. It values imagination. It values the mind far more than the body that can be controlled and domesticated.

i. We are all Brahma. We live in three worlds: undomesticated nature (Prakriti), culture (Sanskrit) which is **domesticated** by others, and our own personalized reality (Brahmanda) based on our own rules.

ii. We are all surrounded by other stories, other truths, each one identifying heroes, villains, victims, saviours and martyrs, justifying **quarrels** over borders and hierarchies.

iii. We all aspire to be **successful,** but rarely do we realize that other people's hell is a consequence of our paradise.

iv. As we grow old, we feed on food of the younger generations but realize how **helpless** we are before death.

v. Nothing terrifies us more than being **exiled** from spaces where we are recognized. We yearn to be identified, evaluated, judged.

In this chapter, we will explore the Brahma within us, constantly fooled by the Brahmas around us into creating our own war zone: the rat race, the dog-eat-dog world, the shark tank.

Escape the Bakasura Trap

Belief ▶ Dependent ▶ **Domesticated**

All humans experience paradise briefly. As infants, all our needs were indulged: We were fed, cleaned, comforted and pampered. It was a life of pleasure and leisure. We had to give nothing in exchange. Nothing was extracted from us. We were not exploited. But then everything changed. It happened gradually.

Tantrums were punished. We were taught to feed ourselves, clean ourselves, comfort ourselves, pamper ourselves. We were told to discipline ourselves, follow rules. We feared we had been cast out of paradise, abandoned. But we were reassured that was not the case. There were rewards if we obeyed, as suggested in Sumerian, Biblical, Greek and Chinese myths. Parents were the first gods who demanded submission. Defiance led to floods and fire, to endless meaningless chores, to disharmony and imbalance. We aspire to be good parents, wonderful parents, control our own creations with our rules, rewarding those who trust us, punishing those who doubt us. We do this for the good of the children. We want to ensure they are never hungry and always safe.

In Hindu myth, humans are born as dependent gods (Devatas), who receive first and can be raised to become dependable gods (Yajamana), who give first. We are born into an ecosystem of exchange, not an ecosystem of submission. But in reality, more often than not, rather than

Step 3 of 3: Feed More, to Sensitize Your 'Belief' Body

participating in exchange, with all its uncertainties, we prefer the certainty of extraction. We extract from parents as children. We extract from children as parents. Instead of Devata (who gets, then gives) and Yajamana (who gives to get), we choose to become Karta (the one who demands) or Karya-Karta (the one who obeys).

In nature, the oak tree produces oak seeds, the goat's child is a goat, the wolf's child is a wolf. But in the human world, the child who grows up to be an obedient sheep can end up parenting a defiant goat, or worse, a wild wolf. No parent can predict what the child will be. So parents mould the imagination of children through stories, symbols and rituals. This is why every tribe has a complex rite of passage, to socialize children, ensure they become part of the tribe where they are safe and dependable. Through these rites and rituals, we are told how to imagine the world (belief), how to conduct ourselves (behaviour) and what to aspire for (business).

Even today, the child raised in American society is nothing like the child raised in Chinese society. Both imagine the world differently. This invisible world they occupy is a combination of natural instincts (Prakriti), cultural conditioning (Sanskriti) and individual creativity (Brahmanda). Everyone struggles between authority and autonomy. We are all naturally dependent. A few of

> Were you obedient as a child? Why do you want your child to be obedient?

us strive to be independent. Most of us are expected to be dependable, responsible and accountable, more for the tribe, less for humanity, and least for ourselves.

Step 3 of 3: Feed More, to Sensitize Your 'Belief' Body

Belief ▶ Dependent ▶ **Quarrels**

In Islamic myth, all humans descend from the same parents: Aadam and Hava. Some children are obedient, hence good, like Habil, and others are disobedient, hence bad, like Qabil. In Christian myth, the same story is told with different names: Adam and Eve, Abel and Cain. In Western myth, a tribe splits because one brother thinks independently and refuses to obey the father's laws. Every tribe, every nation in the West insists they descend from the obedient son, not the disobedient son, hence they are chosen to inherit the earth.

Even Hindu myth speaks of quarrelling brothers. But the reason is different. There is a common father but different mothers. The quarrel is between half-brothers over the inheritance, nothing to do with obeying the rules of the father. It has everything to do with the competitive nature of the mothers. Kashyapa is the father of both the predator and the prey, the eagle (Suparna) and the serpent (Naga), born of two different wives. The eagles are few but powerful; they eat snakes. The serpents are numerous and clever; they trick eagles to leave their nest so they can swallow their eggs. The eagles are supported by the gods (Devas) who live in the sky, and the serpents live along with demons (Asuras) under the ground. The Devas and the Asuras are also two sets of the quarrelling children of Kashyapa, born of two wives. The eagles say the snakes are tricksters. The Asuras say the Devas are tricksters. Hindus since ancient times worship the Devas (tricksters of the sky) and Nagas (tricksters of the earth).

Escape the Bakasura Trap

The Nagas have gems in their head. This is stolen by mongoose for the treasure of Kubera, the Yaksha-king. Kubera is stripped of his treasures and kicked out of his kingdom by Ravana, the Rakshasa-king. Yakshas are hoarders; Rakshasas are raiders. Both have a common father and a different mother. The Rakshasa steals from the Yaksha who steals from the Naga who tricks the Garuda, who eats him, protected by the Devas who trick the Asuras by cornering all the treasures that they together churned out of the ocean of milk.

Mighty sons complain about trickster brothers to the father. Trickster sons seek help from their father to overthrow mighty sons. The wars are endless. The borders and the hierarchies never disappear. They are just redrawn and reorganized. That is because brothers do not seek a fair share. They want to dominate. Every victim is a villain-in-waiting.

> Do you think adult quarrels are real and childhood quarrels are silly?

Step 3 of 3: Feed More, to Sensitize Your 'Belief' Body

Belief ▶ Dependent ▶ **Successful**

The Veda refers to thirty-three Devas, led by Indra. Indra is the most successful of Brahm. But he is never worshipped in a temple. That is because he is an unhappy god. Even though he is the lord of paradise, master of the wish-fulfilling tree, the wish-fulfilling cow and the wish-fulfilling gem with everything that everyone desires, he remains miserable and insecure. His throne keeps wobbling, and he clings to it, afraid of losing everything he has. His paradise is always under siege. He sees predators and rivals everywhere.

Indra refuses to accept the cost of paradise, the consequences of his actions, that create three different kinds of hell. These are not hells of Biblical myth, for the unethical and immoral beings who break God's law. There is no all-powerful God in Hindu myth of this kind. In Hindu myth, the creation of paradise is the cause of hells.

The first hell is Patala, the realm of those tricked and deprived. Here live the Asuras who helped the Devas churn the ocean of milk for all its treasures but were denied any share. The Asuras fight for justice. They seek strength to overpower the Devas who they see as cunning tricksters. The Devas see the Asuras as sore losers, aspiring for things that are not theirs, ambitious out of spite and jealousy.

The second hell is Naraka, the hell of those in debt. When the Devas seek something, they repay debt quickly and remain debt-free. Those bedazzled by the glamour of paradise seek favours from the Devas, without realizing these favours are loans to be repaid. The burden of debt pushes people into Naraka, where they become Pretas, the hungry ghosts. In suffering, the Pretas seek the solace of paradise. They hound the living as they seek a new life, with new circumstances, new parents, new opportunities. But when they get that life, they squander all credit and take more loans and sink deeper and deeper into Naraka. If someone avoids debts and shuns consumption by becoming an ascetic (Tyagi), Indra sends his nymphs to enchant them and seduce them back into the wheel of rebirth.

The third hell is Pitr-loka, the realm of upside-down ancestors, the older generation that impatiently waits for the current generation to make room for the next generation. But Indra will not let go of his throne and his paradise. He drinks the nectar of immortality and refuses to move on. In fact, Indra sees everyone who performs yagna as a rival. He fears if they repay all debts or start giving out loans, they will become Indra themselves and he would be replaced and forgotten.

> **If you pay your own bills, are you not successful? Who is more successful: someone with one private jet or someone with a dozen?**

Step 3 of 3: Feed More, to Sensitize Your 'Belief' Body

Belief ▶ Dependent ▶ **Helpless**

The epic Ramayana is often assumed to be a tale of Ram's greatness. It is in fact the story of Ram from birth to death. The epic Mahabharata is not a tale of war or victory, but the story of Bharata kings, of the Pandavas, Kauravas and Yadavas, from birth to death. There is no climax in these stories. There is only death.

Nature favours the youth. Once they reproduce, it is time to replace them with the next generation. Humans fantasize of a world where they are never replaced. We tell fairy tales of happily-ever-afters, a future without ageing, disease, decay and death. But the hair greys, the skin wrinkles. The wise kings of Buddhist and Jataka tales often give up the household at this stage.

Not all kings are wise. Some cling to the throne. In Greek myths, Cronus eats all his children until he is killed by his son Zeus. Zeus, now king, fears he too will be replaced one day, and so spends all his time keeping humans busy in wars so they do not aspire for the Olympian throne.

In the Mahabharata, when a father called Yayati grows old, rather than retiring gracefully, he asks his sons to give up their youth so that he can stay young. The eldest son refuses and so is disinherited. The youngest son agrees and so is made the heir. By the time the youngest son inherits the throne, he is an old man, his youth having been exploited by his father.

While some Brahmas cannibalize the youth of their sons, others try to fix all problems for their children, leave the world so perfect that there are no problems for the children to solve. In the Ramayana, Dasharatha, who produced four sons with three queens, ends up dying alone, with no son by his side. He wonders what will happen to his kingdom. Despite all efforts, he cannot control the future.

In the Mahabharata, Bhisma, the grand patriarch, has the gift of choosing the time of his death. He refuses to die, as he feels his grandchildren are not quite capable of managing the family inheritance. He is eventually pinned to the ground by arrows, unable to move, forced to witness a brutal war between his grandchildren. He is reminded that the march of time cannot be stopped. Problems that appeared before him and in his lifetime will repeat again, and the new Brahmas will respond as the old Brahmas did. Some will focus on technology to create and distribute food. Others will improve their understanding of hunger. Every rise will have a fall. Every fall will have a rise. Seasons will change. Brahmas will come and go.

> **Do you think stupid and cruel people will not exist after you are no longer the boss?**
> **What did not change after the last boss left?**

Step 3 of 3: Feed More, to Sensitize Your 'Belief' Body

Belief ▶ Dependent ▶ **Stripped**

In Hindu epics, kings are often sent to the forest, stripped of their estates and titles, so they can figure out why kings exist in the first place. In the forest, no plant or animal treats them with respect. They are no different from other organisms, either predator or prey. There is no leisure or labour in the forest, everyone has to fend for their food and security. Nothing can be outsourced.

Ram of the Ramayana is at peace in the forest, as he does not derive his identity from royal status. But the Pandavas of the Mahabharata are miserable. They yearn to be treated as insiders on account of their lineage, but the Kauravas treat them as outsiders. They want to be superiors on account of their talent, but the Kauravas treat them as inferiors. In the forest, they are neither insiders nor outsiders, not superior or inferior. No one seeks respect or gives respect. There are no properties to be inherited, only territories to be defended.

Despite being exiled in the forest for twelve years, despite hiding as servants in a royal household for a year and being witnesses to excesses of the elite, the Pandavas do not see themselves as guardians of culture. They see themselves as victims, fighting for justice. Kingdom for them remains property, not responsibility. They want to fight the Kauravas to take back what is theirs by right. They want to be Indras. It is the recurring Deva–Asura battle once more, brothers

Escape the Bakasura Trap

fighting brothers over inheritance, the tricksters and the talented accusing each other of being immortal and unethical.

When compromise fails, both sides seek the support of the Yadavas in their war efforts. Balarama, the elder Yadava, is disgusted by the refusal to compromise and share. He refuses to engage with either. Krishna, the younger Yadava, decides to help both. He offers either his army (Narayani) or himself, unarmed (Narayan). He gives first choice to the Pandavas. This annoys the Kauravas who as superiors are not used to accepting leftovers. The Pandavas are overwhelmed with gratitude at being offered first choice, as no one before has granted them such respect.

The Pandavas choose Krishna, much to the relief of the Kauravas, who wanted the army in the first place. The Kauravas felt they were entitled to Krishna's support as they were insiders, members of the same clan, with common ancestors. Neither the Pandavas nor the Kauravas saw the interaction as a yagna.

> When have you felt unrecognized by those who once admired you? Have you deliberately ignored someone to hurt them?

Krishna's enemy, Jarasandha, had been defeated with Pandava help. So Krishna was obliged to help the Pandavas. He had no such obligation with the Kauravas. The Pandavas did not see Krishna as a Devata repaying his debt. The Kauravas did not see Krishna as a Yajamana who was

Step 3 of 3: Feed More, to Sensitize Your 'Belief' Body

placing them in debt. The Kauravas and the Pandavas were products of a feudal society, based on extraction rather than exchange, where no one bothered with balance sheets. As is belief, so is behaviour, so is business.

Belief ▶ Independent

In Hindu myth, Shiva is the destroyer. Not of villains, demons or the disobedient. But of his own hunger and fear. We all have a Shiva inside us, one who does not have to live life in the pursuit of food or security. This is the hermit way, an option to the life of endless comparisons and pursuits.

i. A Shiva begins with **restraint** and moderation determining what is enough and what is surplus, avoiding paradise with the awareness of hell.

ii. A Shiva strives to be **indifferent** to praise and insult, so is at peace in paradise as well as hell.

iii. A Shiva knows he attracts the **opportunist** who see him as an easy source of food, gullible enough to give without asking anything in exchange.

iv. A Shiva knows he attracts the **paranoid** and the fragile who see him as a refuge but eventually get frustrated when he does not give them the attention and validation they need.

v. A Shiva knows there is no escaping the hungry and the frightened. He **empathizes** with offerings of knowledge, digesting which is never easy.

This chapter is about the Shiva within us who seeks independence from the forest of hunger and fear. We all discover eventually that no mountain is too cold and no cave too deep to escape from those addicted to food and security.

Step 3 of 3: Feed More, to Sensitize Your 'Belief' Body

Belief ▶ Independent ▶ **Restrained**

Parables draw attention to the consequences of greed. The golden touch of Midas turns his daughter into a statue. The ravenous Erysichthon sold his children to buy food. Why were they greedy? Greek myth blames the Olympian gods. Midas is a victim of a prank played by Dionysus. Erysichthon is cursed by Demeter to cut her sacred tree.

In Christian myth, greed is sin, the outcome of free will, the refusal to follow laws of the one true God, succumbing to the temptation of the Devil. In Chinese myths, greed is natural. It is restrained by respect for ancestors and countered by various social forces designed to shame the unvirtuous. Nature does not tolerate parasites and so the Chinese sage who knows the Dao knows that the greedy will eventually be stopped.

In Hindu myth, greed is the result of ignorance. We eventually learn that paradise will never end our hunger. Gautama saw decay and death around him, grey hair and wrinkles on those who were once young and beautiful, and decided to withdraw from society. He gave up his household, became a hermit. He began to fast but soon became so weak that he could not walk or concentrate. The only thought in his mind then was about food. He collapsed and was nursed back to health by a milkmaid. That is when Gautama realized that we are tempted by that which we shun. The hermit who tries to control his senses and refuses to participate in the

Escape the Bakasura Trap

yagna is enchanted by damsels sent by Indra, and by the pitiful cries of those who depend on him. He ends up deep in debt. The point is moderation. This was the path of the Buddha. And the way to do that was by paying attention to the measuring scale.

Buddha's cousin, the handsome Ananda, was obsessed with his wife. So Buddha took him to Swarga where he saw gorgeous damsels who yearned for him. Thereafter, he found his wife uninteresting. Buddha then took Ananda to hell where he saw ghosts of men longing for his wife. Suddenly his wife seemed beautiful again.

Ananda stopped desiring his wife when he realized others desired him. He resumed desiring his wife when he realized she was desirable to others. We exist in a number line. There is always something better above and worse below. We can keep climbing endlessly or going down endlessly. The quest for paradise makes us devalue what we have. The sight of hell makes us value what we have. When we look at the addictions of paradise and the miseries of hell, we identify what we need to be content. Everything else becomes surplus.

> **Do you stay away from people who constantly compare and compete? Do you stay away from people who need your help?**

Step 3 of 3: Feed More, to Sensitize Your 'Belief' Body

Belief ▶ Independent ▶ **Indifferent**

In Buddhism, desire is a demon who Gautama defeats. In Hinduism, desire is a god who Shiva burns. Shiva smears his body with the ash. The world around Shiva becomes desolate – devoid of hunger. Rivers freeze. Nothing germinates. No plant craves for sunlight or water. No animal yearns for flesh. There is desire to chase opportunity. There is no threat to run away from.

King Rishabha saw how Indra tried to cover up the death of a nymph in paradise. Realizing death is inevitable, even in the realm of alleged immortals, he renounced his kingdom and walked the path of the Jina, those who conquer the craving for paradise. He did not shun the world. He sought to overcome his hunger. He fasted not to avoid food but to train his body until eating was no longer a craving or a habit. As the days passed, he ate lesser and lesser food until hunger became a choice, not an involuntary physiological need.

The sage Vardhamana sat in meditation, eyes shut, mind withdrawn. A cowherd wondered if he had seen his missing cows. When Vardhamana did not reply, the cowherd felt he was hiding something. So he pierced the ears of Vardhamana with thorns and placed a dead snake around him that attracted ants which bit into Vardhamana's flesh. Vardhamana said nothing. Some merchants who saw the bleeding ears and inflamed skin of Vardhamana rushed to help him. They got doctors to remove the thorns, the ants, the snake and apply soothing ointment. Vardhamana said nothing. He did not curse the cowherd or bless the merchants. There was no debt of consumption or credit of feeding. The balance sheet was clean. Vardhamana observed how nature is full of causeless cruelty and kindness. If one outgrows hunger and fear, one feels no need to react to kindness or cruelty. Vardhamana came to be known as Mahavira, greater than rana-vira who defends the weak and daan-vira who feeds the hungry. He was maha-vira, who conquers his own mind.

A hero (vira) seeks his own glory. A greater hero (maha-vira) is one who revels in other people's glory. Hanuman was once asked why he did not defeat Ravana and rescue Sita himself. Hanuman replied because Ram did not ask him to. It was Ram's story, not his. It was about Ram's glory, not his.

> **Can you be happy without your phone, alone in an empty room? Can you be happy with people who are always unhappy?**

Likewise, Ram could have openly challenged and defeated Vali. But he killed Vali secretly from the bushes, while Vali was fighting Sugriva, because that is what Sugriva asked him to do. It was Sugriva's story. Not Ram's. Ram was being Maha-vira so that Sugriva could be the vira, who defeated his alpha brother.

Step 3 of 3: Feed More, to Sensitize Your 'Belief' Body

Belief ▶ Independent ▶ **Opportunist**

Modern gurus claim to be hermits, like Shiva. They even wear mendicant costumes to display their renunciant status – ash on the forehead, long, matted hair, beads around their neck. But unlike Shiva, they seek endless attention and validation from followers. In exchange, they give followers the assurance that they are not hoarders like Kubera or raiders like Ravana. Thus, gurus who renounce the world end up creating beehives, where they are the queen bee and their followers the worker bees collecting honey for the cult.

But Shiva seeks no company. Kubera comes to him seeking sanctuary as he has been driven out of Lanka by his half-brother Ravana. Shiva shows him the Naga serpents around his neck. They have no jewel on their hood. They were all stolen by Kubera's mongoose for Kubera's treasury. With no jewels on their head, they were no longer attractive to anyone; they were safe. Shiva asked Kubera to give away his wealth, become unattractive, and so safe. But Kubera could not do that. Without his treasures, he would not be envied or worshipped. What would he be then? Kubera sought safety with his treasures. Shiva offered peace and contentment stemming from losing interest in jewels.

Kubera offered Shiva's son, the elephant-headed Ganesha, all the food he could eat. Ganesha ate everything in Kubera's kitchen and kept asking for more. Finally, Kubera realized that food does not take away hunger. It increases addiction

Escape the Bakasura Trap

to food. Shiva destroys hunger itself. That is why the snake around Ganesha's belly does not chase Ganesha's pet rat who does not nibble on the sweets and fruits on Ganesha's palm. No one is hungry in Shiva's abode. When there are no predators, there is no prey. Even the lion lays with the lamb, as the Bible says.

From afar, Shiva looks prosperous, enjoying the mountain winds in summer, enjoying the warmth of funeral pyres in winter, too confident to bother with borders or hierarchies. His confidence caught the eye of Ravana. He wanted what Shiva had. So he decided to pick up Shiva's snow-clad mountain, Kailash, and take it down south to his island kingdom of Lanka. But the further south he went, the heavier the mountain became. It was the burden of debt that comes with every act of consumption.

Ravana assumed he could take wealth from Shiva without having to give up his power. Just as Kubera assumed he could take power from Shiva without having to give up his wealth. In the realm of the content, the frightened feel safe only if they stop hoarding and the hungry feel satisfied if they stop seeking. While both Ravana and Kubera venerate Shiva, they saw him as a source of endless wealth and power to indulge their endless hunger

> Have you met people who think kindness is weakness? Have you allowed people to take advantage of you?

Escape the Bakasura Trap

Belief ▶ Independent ▶ **Paranoid**

An Asura, angry with the Devas, obtained from Shiva a boon by which he could reduce anyone to a heap of ash by touching their head. Shiva gave him the boon, so he became renowned as Bhasma-asura or ash-demon. Everyone now feared him. But not Shiva, who feared nothing as he desired nothing. This made Bhasmasura nervous. He feared Shiva would one day overpower him to help the Devas. So he decided to touch Shiva's head and destroy him forever. He began pursuing Shiva, when he was distracted by the sight of a damsel. He offered the damsel his love, but the damsel frowned in disgust. When asked for a reason, the damsel said he had worms on his head. So Bhasmasura touched his head to remove the worms and was reduced to ash.

If Bakasura embodies the one who is always hungry, Bhasmasura embodies the one who is always frightened. Bakasura never feels satisfied. Bhasmasura never feels safe. Both are very similar. Hungry Bakasura is always frightened of starvation. Frightened Bhasmasura is always hungry for security. He feels threatened constantly. He is fragile, oversensitive, feeling disrespected when denied attention. Bakasura seeks opportunity everywhere. If you are not food or feeder, you are rival. Bhasmasura seeks oppression everywhere. If you are not the oppressed, if you do not support or agree with him, you are the oppressor. If Bakasura is the capitalist seeking endless growth, Bhasmasura is the socialist who seeks endless revolutions. They turn even the hermit's

Step 3 of 3: Feed More, to Sensitize Your 'Belief' Body

heaven into a battleground. They see victims everywhere and so even those who are indifferent are perceived as villains.

If we are ambitious all the time, we are in the Bakasura trap, trying to invalidate other truths with our own. If we are angry all the time, upset with the way the world functions, we are Bhasmasura, delighting in breaking down other people's truth. If one considers this carefully, we realize Bakasuras are Bhasmasuras, the hungry are also the angry, wondering why the prey is constantly running away. When people shun us, it is often because we have not realized how scary and inedible we have become.

If we are Shiva, we will attract everyone despite our indifference. We will attract the hungry who think we are gullible. We will also attract the frightened and fragile who see us as safe. Both will get angry when they realize we are not the source of what they seek.

> Have you met people who think there is oppression everywhere? Have you met people who want you to admire them all the time, and not give them any criticism?

Belief ▶ Independent ▶ **Empathy**

Buddhism speaks of a prince who walks away from his wife, his son, his father and his kingdom, and becomes a hermit. His focus is the self. His path is solitary. The rest does not matter. He walks the higher path of wisdom. This is much like Maslow's hierarchy taught in schools, where it is all about the self: self-preservation, self-propagation, self-indulgence, self-security, self-actualization, self-realization. The other is not even considered. The other benefits from the wisdom of the self. But is the other seeking that wisdom? Is the self offering food that the other is not hungry for?

The other is who we consume. The other is who we decide not to consume. The other is who seeks to consume us and the one who is left starving. Buddha welcomes his father, his mother, his wife and his son to walk his path. He refuses to return to the household. For the one giving knowledge, the other is the student. Giving food to the hungry and power to the insecure is easy. Giving knowledge to the curious is easy. But not all students are curious.

Demand for knowledge is low. We seek skills to get more wealth and power. Few seek knowledge of the self. But knowledge of the self is incomplete and incorrect without the knowledge of the other.

In Hindu mythology, Shiva, the ash-smeared naked ascetic, lives atop a mountain of stone covered with snow, where there

Step 3 of 3: Feed More, to Sensitize Your 'Belief' Body

is no flora or fauna. He is sought not only by opportunist and paranoid demons, but also by the Goddess. She makes Shiva her husband, sets up a home for him, complete with a kitchen, armoury and children.

I do not need it, says Shiva. I want it, says the Goddess. And they want it, pointing to the hungry and the frightened who live below in the valley of despair. Her food is for them. Her weapons are for them. Her children are for them: Kartikeya will protect the weak, Ganesha will feed the strong. She wants Shiva to open his eyes to her hunger and her fear, the hunger and fear of those around, have empathy, expand his sense of self to include the others around him.

Shiva once got angry with the clanging of utensils in the kitchen. He told the Goddess to stop cooking so he could concentrate. The Goddess disappeared. Soon the mountains were filled with the howling of ghosts. Feed us, feed us, they cried. That is when Shiva realized he could concentrate in silence because the Goddess fed the ghosts. He may not need food, but others do. His truth was not the only truth. So he went in search of the Goddess and found her in Kashi. He begged her for food. Not for himself, but for others.

And so, in Buddhism and Jainism, goddesses were included. She is Tara in Buddhism. She is the Yakshini, of many names, in Jainism. They hold fruits in one hand and weapons in the other. They provide and protect the hungry and the frightened, and patiently wait for them, over endless lifetimes, to become curious and fill their 'business' body with the knowledge that will help them open their eyes to other people's hungers, fears and truths.

In Jainism and Buddhism, the hungry and frightened householder becomes the generous and resilient householder before he becomes the detached hermit, which is the ultimate goal. In Hinduism, the path is circular. The unhappy householder is truly a content hermit when he returns to the household, not to eat but to feed. Shiva's food is knowledge. Few receive it. Very few digest it. More often than not the knowledge becomes property, hoarded and defended more than consumed. This is why, very often, the knowledgeable are not wise.

One day, Shiva was explaining the Veda to his wife. She yawned. Angry, Shiva told her she was not fit to be his student. Go away, he said. So she left. Without the Goddess to ask him questions or seek clarifications, Shiva had no one to speak to. A teacher is useless without a student, he realized. He longed for his perfect student, his dear wife. He went looking for her and found her by the sea, living as a fisherwoman. To get her back as his wife, he had to woo her. For that he had to learn fishing and impress her with his skills. Learning the new skill was not easy. It was boring and tiresome. Shiva realized that being a student is different

> Can you see the insecurities of the glamorous and the invisible people?
> Do feel guilty when you see beggars?

Step 3 of 3: Feed More, to Sensitize Your 'Belief' Body

from being a teacher. He empathized with the yawn of his wife. He finally learnt fishing and manged to bring her back home as his wife, his perfect student. More importantly, he realized he had to be patient with students, allow them to learn at their own pace. And allow them to yawn when they find something boring, even if the teacher thinks the subject is most interesting. It is a feedback not on the subject, but on the art of teaching.

Escape the Bakasura Trap

Belief ▶ Dependable

Vishnu is the preserver as he restores the exchange rejected by Shiva and exploited by Brahma. This is the householder way, one where the focus is on the other. This is different from Brahma, the householder whose focus is the self, as in Maslow's famous hierarchy.

i. A Vishnu is like a parent who **playacts** (leela) with children, turning every imaginary war zone (Rana-Bhoomi) into a fun zone (Ranga-Bhoomi), nudging the dependent baby to discover independence by being the dependable adult.

ii. A Vishnu **repays** all that he owes. He is never in debt. He cannot be tricked by the opportunist or ensnared by the paranoid.

iii. A Vishnu **reclaims** all loans. There is no escape from responsibility and accountability. There is no writing off what is owed. Those who eat must be eaten.

iv. A Vishnu uses all his surplus to **reinvest.** This is not lending, which is impatient. Investment is about voluntary returns. They are unpredictable but inevitable. Those who are fed must eventually learn to feed. There is no hurry, there is no escape in the wheel of infinite rebirths.

v. A Vishnu knows everyone ultimately wants to feel wanted, **desired,** valued, but on their own terms, not for

Step 3 of 3: Feed More, to Sensitize Your 'Belief' Body

what we have but for who we are. Those who are valued always pay it forward.

In this chapter, we will explore the Vishnu within us. He is often mistakenly described as a saviour, but Vishnu sees through the gaze of adoration. He is not fooled by tricksters or impressed by the talented. All he cares about is the yagna. Helping the hungry Devata who eats first become the content Yajamana who feeds first because he can see the hunger and fear of the other.

Belief ▶ Dependable ▶ **Playacting**

In Western and Eastern myth, rules matter. Following God's law brings peace. The Devil of Biblical myth defies. The hero of Greek myth defies. The Chinese court expected children to obey parents, women to obey men, the young to obey the old, students to obey teachers, juniors to obey seniors. Those in positions of power were expected to display virtue for balance and harmony. It is all about the 'behavioural' body.

Hindu myth does not care for the 'behavioural' but focuses on 'belief'. How do we see the other? Sadly, the former is measurable and more popular. We are happy with alignment and obedience. But Vishnu knows that all rule-followers are not good and all rule-breakers are not bad. Why you follow or break rules is far more important than the act itself.

In the epic Ramayana, Vishnu is Ram who follows the rules. Ravana is the villain who breaks the rules. In the Mahabharata, Krishna breaks the rules. The villain is Duryodhana who follows the rules.

Ram and Krishna have no aspiration or ambition. They are content. They work to help those around them. By contrast, Ravana and Duryodhana are only interested in feeding themselves, even if their kingdoms are destroyed and their subjects killed. All four are kings, but Vishnu's avatars exist to feed the other and get the other to repay the debt. That

Step 3 of 3: Feed More, to Sensitize Your 'Belief' Body

exchange is dharma. The kings who fight Vishnu are kings who would eat rather than feed. This extraction is adharma.

For Ram and Krishna, Ravana and Duryodhana are not evil. They are overgrown children who cling to toys and do not let others play. They do not take their responsibility as kings seriously. They have no qualms about causing the destruction of Lanka and Hastinapur to get what they want. They are petulant and over-smart children. Forcing them to obey will only make them more defiant or more subversive. The resentment will fester. Behaviour is not the point. They need to learn to see the other. They need to overcome their addiction to food, their paranoid delusions.

Kings exist only in culture. In Buddhist lore, kings were appointed to ensure property rights and to prevent property fights. Kings were given weapons to deter thieves, raiders and usurpers. In Hindu myth, kings were created to ensure no one plunders the earth or exploits people, no one grabs more and gives less. The king is a cowherd who ensures the earth-cow is not exploited.

Kings do not exist only to feed. And subjects do not exist only to be fed. Everyone is answerable to the earth. Everyone needs to see the balance sheet, learn to repay debts, reinvest surplus, reclaim loans and replay with resilience.

> **Have you given a false compliment to get people to be nice and kind? Do you need a reason to be nice and kind?**

Belief ▶ Dependable ▶ **Repay**

We are beneficiaries of other people's investments. So we are all born in debt. We owe our parents, our family, our culture and nature. We are raised by consuming and we need to spend the rest of our life repaying what we consumed. There is no winning or losing for Vishnu, just repaying in order to be free.

Vishnu once took the form of a small fish and asked humans to save him from the big fish. The human who did it became Manu, the father of human civilization, for in a civilized world the strong help the weak. Here, Manu earned credit and Vishnu was in debt. Years later, a flood threatened to submerge Manu's world. That is when Vishnu appeared as a big fish and rescued Manu who had taken refuge in a boat. Vishnu thus repaid the debt and Manu benefited from his credit.

As Ram, Vishnu is the eldest son of the royal family. So he enjoys the privileges of being a prince. But he never takes it as entitlement. He has no ambition to be king. So he gives it away to his brother, Bharat, when asked to do so by his father, bearing no grudge. Bharat refuses to accept the crown obtained by his mother's trickery. The king may have given her a boon, but by asking for the crown, she is misusing her credit, satisfying her own hunger at the cost of the kingdom. Neither Ram nor Bharat aspire to be kings. They aspire to fulfil their roles as members of royalty. They are responsible

Step 3 of 3: Feed More, to Sensitize Your 'Belief' Body

for the kingdom, never letting anyone question the integrity of the family name. This showcasing of adulthood is what makes the Ramayana special.

As Krishna is the youngest son of a cowherd family, he has no responsibilities. He enjoys being fed butter by the milkmaids of Gokula. He even steals from them, irritating them. But all this playful indulgence puts Vishnu in debt. He repays by saving the village from torrential rains and forest fires, by playing the flute at night, inviting all the women to dance around him at night in the dark forest without any fear. They take away his hunger for affection and he takes away their fear of exploitation. Liberated from all debts, Krishna leaves the village eventually. The milkmaids protest. But Vishnu will not let them be dependent. He will not turn them into hungry ghosts in Naraka, pining for Swarga. He wants them to be dependable, invest in others and enjoy the returns.

Indradyumna donated many cows in his lifetime. Cows are a Sanskrit metaphor for a source of livelihood, unfortunately taken literally by politicians. By providing livelihood for others, Indradyumna repaid all his loans, and began accumulating a lot of credit. This ensured him a place in paradise. All those he gave cows to eventually died. With no beneficiary left, he wondered why he was still in paradise. That is when he was told that he had given so many cows that the

> Have you helped people who were nasty to you in the past? Have you been helped by nasty people?

dust they kicked up while leaving his cowshed had created a depression. It got filled with rainwater. It became a lake, home to many plants and animal species. It was still home to turtles who were named after him. And those he had given cows to had also donated more cows, creating more ponds, more ecosystems, no turtles. Indradyumna's stay in paradise was assured because those he nourished were paying it forward.

Step 3 of 3: Feed More, to Sensitize Your 'Belief' Body

Belief ▶ Dependable ▶ **Reclaim**

A blink for humans is a lifespan for an insect. So we do not bother with insects. But we expect Indra, Brahma, Vishnu, Shiva and Devi to save us even though the human lifespan is equal to the blink of an Indra; Indra's lifespan is the blink of a Brahma; a Brahma's lifespan is the blink of a Vishnu; a blink of Shiva is the lifespan of a Vishnu; a blink of Devi is the lifespan of a Shiva. This is because every human imagines himself or herself to be special, with the right to consume everything and everyone, endlessly, feeling like a victim when not allowed to do it.

Those who are born into privilege, like Duryodhana of the Mahabharata, and those who succeed in cornering privilege, like Ravana of the Ramayana, continue to behave like victims. They want to extract more from life rather than be Devatas who have to repay those whose investment made their privilege possible.

In the Ramayana, Ram helps Sugriva become king by killing Vali. He then expects Sugriva to repay the debt by helping him rescue Sita. Ram reclaims this debt.

At Kurukshetra, after the Pandavas defeat the Kauravas, Bhima wonders if he is the reason for victory or if it is Arjuna. Ask the head atop the hill, says Krishna. The head belonged to a warrior who had died on his way to the war and wanted to see the outcome. So the gods had placed his head on a hill that overlooked the battlefield. He had a different line of sight. To everyone's surprise, the head saw neither Bhima nor Arjuna, neither the Kauravas nor the Pandavas, neither the mighty nor the meek. He saw kings killing each other and the earth drinking their blood. She was eating those who had eaten her. She was reclaiming the debt humanity owed her.

Bhima and Arjuna realized the war was not about justice or their rights. It was not a competition to see who was the better warrior. It was all about treating the earth with dignity, by getting rid of those who plunder her, drinking her milk rather than distributing it. The Kauravas were too busy fighting their rivals to focus on their responsibility as kings. And the Pandavas, despite the proximity to Krishna, did not pay any attention to kingship either. They were too busy wallowing in victimhood to bother with accountability and responsibility.

> **How do you feel when someone constantly reminds you of how they helped you in the past? Have you reminded people of their ingratitude?**

Step 3 of 3: Feed More, to Sensitize Your 'Belief' Body

Belief ▶ Dependable ▶ **Reinvest**

In nature, success is about staying alive. Failure is about dying of starvation or being killed by a predator. To survive you outrun the predator or the prey, as the case may be. In culture, we can create walls and keep out all plants and animals that can hurt us. We can domesticate all plants and animals we want to eat. So theoretically, humans as a species can be very happy, using our imagination that brings forth fabulous technology. But that is not what happens.

Humans seek the pleasure of leisure. We get other humans to labour. The weak are labourers. Women are labourers. Juniors are labourers. That is not enough, amongst those with pleasure and leisure, there is a race: who gets more pleasure, who gets more leisure, who listens to whom?

Indra is at the top of the pile – everyone listens to him, and he has access to all pleasure and leisure. That makes him worthy of worship. But he fears losing his exalted position. And he gets bored easily. He needs to compare and compete to feel richer and mightier than the other. This gives meaning to his life. It is all about extracting, not exchange. When asked to exchange, he uses trickery to ensure he always gets more. Those around him wait for him to fail. They wait for him to die. They worship him only in fear, or because they want something from him.

Escape the Bakasura Trap

Some are Indras at birth. Some become Indra over time. All Indras enjoy being envied and feared. His ecosystem is an unhappy one. In Swarga, the apsara dances for Indra's pleasure. Pleasure is a weapon designed to destroy the resolve of hermits. Indra only takes pleasure; he does not give pleasure. He does not know the pleasure of giving pleasure.

A Vishnu heaven is about giving pleasure. In Jain and Buddhist mythology, kings give up the household and kingdom for peace. They become hermits. In Hindu mythology, Vishnu becomes Mohini, the enchantress, and approaches Shiva, and asks him the secret of giving pleasure. Shiva says it is in the giving of pleasure. Then why don't you, asks Mohini. So Shiva becomes the householder, giving pleasure to the Goddess, just as Vishnu as Krishna plays the flute and gets the cows to offer milk voluntarily, his heaven of cows (Go-loka). Here, the exploited cows do not wish to drink the blood of kings who exploit them as the earth did at Kurukshetra. They give pleasure (milk) to those who give them pleasure (music). A cycle of reinvestment is created.

> What have you invested in to make life of strangers better a hundred years from today? Should people invest in infrastructure or forests?

Step 3 of 3: Feed More, to Sensitize Your 'Belief' Body

Belief ▶ Dependable ▶ **Desirability**

There is no climax in this world. There is eternal replay. Rule-breakers and rule-followers. The talented, the defiant, the trickster, the pretender. Vishnu has seen it all. There are no surprises, shocks or accidents. Food will never take away hunger. Power will never take away fear. We will waste lifetimes eating, extracting, exploiting, raiding, trading, hoarding, rebelling, scolding and punishing. Peace will only come when we realize the meaning of existence. Our secret desire to be consumed.

Value comes from being eaten. The sun is valuable because plants see it as food. The plants are valuable because herbivores see them as food. Herbivores are valuable as carnivores see them as food. Plants and animals are valuable because humans see them as resources. What makes humans valuable? Who consumes humans?

As infants we feel valued when we are the object of attention. But as we grow up that attention wanes. So we offer goods and services to get the attention back. We do not like unwanted attention. That is violation. We want attention on our own terms. So we engage in exchange.

Over time, we become undesirable. We are wanted only for the goods, services and ideas we have to offer. We are envied for our hoard of goods, services and ideas. Never valued for who we are. We long for the attention. That attention grants us meaning. It is the reason we love dogs who are so excited to see us, even if we treat them badly. Wanted by no one, desired by no one, we die meaningless lives, surrounded by debtors and creditors. This was true before. This is true today. This will be true tomorrow.

Vishnu knows this. So he does not simply feed the hungry. He makes the hungry feel like they are food, the source of his meaning. He gives the attention we long for. He beams when he sees us like newborns who beam at the sight of the parent, just enough so that it does feel like dependence. Vishnu knows that in an ecosystem, organisms thrive not just because they eat, but also because they are desired. To be wanted is as important as to get what one wants.

Only the content can see the desire of the other to be desired. That is what makes a Vishnu initiate the yagna for the hungry Devata. He praises them and invites them for a meal. He says 'Svaha!' and wants them to say, 'Tathastu!' All he wants is to reinvest the surplus on more hungry souls, patiently waiting for the returns that accrue over lifetimes. He has no hurry.

The returns of the past come in the present. The returns of the present will come in the future. His ocean of milk is endless and always overflowing. Wherever he goes in the jungle of hunger and fear, there is always mangal (the delight of meaning).

Step 3 of 3: Feed More, to Sensitize Your 'Belief' Body

A Vishnu always brings opportunity and meaning wherever he goes. He reduces threats and does not let anyone feel invalidated.

In the Ramayana, Ram strokes the back of squirrels who carry pebbles to build the bridge across the sea to Lanka, to help Ram rescue his wife who is trapped there. The boulder-carrying monkeys wonder why Ram is appreciating their miniscule efforts. Surely the contribution of boulders is greater than the contribution of pebbles, objectively speaking. Ram says that subjectively, the squirrels are contributing as much as the monkeys. Surely, all contributions need to be appreciated. Wisdom is about seeing the world from the other's point of view.

> Do you bring fortune and joy wherever you go? Do people feel safe and nourished when they see you?

Bhima's Contentment

Bhima is fed by Hidimbi

After winning the war, after ruling the kingdom for a long time, the Pandavas decided it was time to make way for the next generation. So they gave up all possessions and made their way up the mountains, hoping to enter paradise and live with the gods.

Along the way, Draupadi slipped and fell to her death, followed by the younger three Pandavas, one by one. Bhima wondered why. Yudhishthira did not turn back to save them. He kept walking, giving explanations for their fall. Sahadeva, Nakula and Arjuna died because they were arrogant, vain and insecure despite their privilege and success. Their wife died because she favoured Arjuna over her other husbands.

It dawned on Bhima that his competition for Draupadi's affection was a wasted effort; she loved someone else. Unfortunately for Draupadi, Arjuna would only obey his elder brothers, not her. When Draupadi wanted to kill her abuser, she needed someone who would defy Yudhishthira. So she used Bhima, who was ever willing to please his wife and who resented his elder brother's authority and misplaced morality.

Bhima was used to being used. It was he who killed the Asuras of the forest who threatened his family. It was he who killed Jarasandha, tyrant of Magadha, enabling the coronation of Yudhishthira. It was he who killed the Kauravas and reclaimed Pandava land. It was only he who had sought to avenge Draupadi's repeated humiliation, indifferent to model codes of conduct. Yet his victory was always described as Pandava victory. He was eclipsed by his family, his individual achievements diluted by the collective.

When Bhima slipped and fell, he did not get angry when Yudhishthira did not turn around to save him. He saw Yudhishthira. He saw his beliefs beyond his behaviour. He knew Yudhishthira was striving to do what he was told hermits do – let go. Yudhishthira had no great skills, so he tried to earn respect by being obedient, by impressing elders, parents and teachers by being earnest about following the rules. His privileges came from his accident of birth that made him the eldest son. He needed Arjuna to find him a powerful wife. He needed Arjuna to burn the forest of Khandava to build his city. He needed Bhima to crush his enemies. With no great capability or achievement of his own, at the very least, Yudhishthira could justify his privilege by doing what others expected him to do.

With his eyes on the rules, Yudhishthira never saw the hungers and fears of those around him. The one time Yudhishthira had indulged his own hunger, for gambling, he lost everything he had and was abused by all. Never again would he take risks. The violent price of kingship disgusted him. He wanted to be a hermit. But the words of Bhima motivated him to his role as the eldest son of a royal family, much like Ram of the Ramayana. Even Arjuna needed the words of Krishna to take up arms in Kurukshetra, take back what was rightfully his family's. Bhima needed no such motivation from others. He knew it was his duty, as Pandu's son, to be king. He knew it was his duty, as Kunti's son, to fight for his family inheritance. He knew it was his duty, as Draupadi's husband, to defend her and avenge her violation.

On becoming king, Yudhishthira was determined to be the ideal ruler, like Ram of the Ramayana, bound by rules, detached and dispassionate like Yama, the god of death. He knew why Bhima and his other brothers and his wife were not being allowed to enter paradise. He could do nothing about their balance sheet. He was determined to enter paradise, like a god, the reward for respecting the rules. He even insisted a dog that followed him be granted entry to Swarga. But then he discovered the ghosts of the Kauravas in paradise, not the ghosts of the Pandavas, and that made Yudhishthira furious at the injustice of it all.

As he was falling, Yudhishthira said that Bhima was being denied entry into Swarga for his gluttony. He who overate all his life would be eaten in his next life. In Naraka, Bhima learnt that the Kauravas had risen to Swarga. However, unlike Yudhishthira, he was not outraged.

Yudhishthira, the rule-follower, was upset because he felt paradise was a reward for rule-followers, not rule-breakers. He had not forgiven the Kauravas despite killing them in battle and taking over their property. Yudhishthira forgot paradise is for those with credit and hell is for those in debt. Just as the Pandavas had landed up in hell burdened by leftover debt, having enjoyed all credit on earth, the Kauravas had risen to paradise to enjoy leftover credit, as their debts were wiped out the moment they were killed in battle. The Kauravas may not have fed the Pandavas, but they did feed many others, especially Karna, giving him the respect and dignity he yearned for.

Bhima's Contentment

Karna gave charity. He put others in debt. He did not invest; he did not give credit; he did not help people repay debts; he did not reclaim loans given, and so let people suffer the burden of debt. So he too landed in Naraka. There he saw the four Pandavas who were in hell for extracting power by repeatedly insulting Karna as a charioteer's son, stripping him of power. Karna knew the four were his brothers. The four knew Karna was their elder brother. Must one be an elder brother to get respect? Is a charioteer's son not deserving of respect? Would Karna have been charitable if he was not repeatedly abused as a charioteer's son, desperate for respect?

In the last chapter, Yudhishthira, the beneficiary of so much credit and privilege, the great rule-follower, the successful one, was unable to accept the balance sheet of the gods. He saw the Kauravas as the villains, rule-breakers to be punished, not cousins who he could forgive. Ram blamed the balance sheet, not his stepmother Kaikeyi, for his misfortune. Yudhishthira could not do the same. The eldest Pandava could not forgive his insecure cousins. Just as the Kauravas could not share with their hungry cousins.

Did Bhima forgive the Kauravas? Or did he like Yudhishthira resent the Kaurava rise to Indra's paradise to enjoy the little credit they had?

There is no objective answer to this question. For such is the nature of art, literature and storytelling. But we can speculate and by doing so expand our mind with ideas.

The key to the speculation is Bhima's first wife, Hidimbi, sister of Bakasura. She had revealed the secret of growing with contentment long before Hanuman confronted Bhima's conceit. But no one listened. Perhaps because she was a woman, or worse, the sister of Baka, Hidimba, Jata and other demons.

Hidimbi fed her brother's killer and his family. In exchange, she wanted Bhima not to kill any more of the forest dwellers who grabbed food since they did not know any better. She protected and provided for everyone in the forest. She wanted nothing for herself. She was self-sufficient. Around her was Vaikuntha, the realm of abundance, where everyone feeds the other. However, not even the narrator of the Mahabharata referred to Hidimbi as the first daughter-in-law of the Pandava clan, the one who came before Draupadi. Hidimbi was never more than a side character in Bhima's story. Yet she never saw herself as a victim. Self-sufficient people do not seek other people's approval or admiration. She was generous in her caretaking and resilient when ignored. She perhaps was indifferent to the fact that in the years to come, she would be worshipped as a goddess, adored in her forest on the slopes of the Himalayas.

Bhima's Contentment

Kunti rejected Hidimbi's heaven as she wanted more for her children. She reminded the Pandavas of their inheritance, that they were obliged to consume. She refused to write off the loan. This was not ambition, she argued. This was dharma, reclaiming dues. Her children did create the paradise of Indraprastha, aptly named, as it was surrounded by jealous forces who resented Pandava success. Yudhishthira was enchanted into the gambling hall. He refused to listen to good sense. His hunger for greater thrill and victory marked the end of the family fortune. Thus, the war zone was re-established. It was established once again when Bhima could not outgrow his need to hurt his blind old uncle who had lost all his sons. The bait to punish predators and rivals is too great for those who imagine themselves as victims.

Bakasura's world Kaurava's world	Bhima's world	Hidimbi's world Krishna's world
If I do not eat, I will be eaten	Feed the insiders	I can feed myself
Do they give you resources?	Eat the outsiders	I will feed those who fed me
Do you give them services?	Feed the superiors	I will feed the hungry
Do they give you services?	Eat the inferiors	I will teach the hungry to feed themselves
		I will wait patiently for others to feed me

If, at the moment of death, Bhima stopped seeing the Kauravas as villains, having understood their hunger and fear, he would surely have reached Vaikuntha, the heaven of contentment. He would have finally seen Hidimbi there.

Contentment is not about being reaching a target. It is not an afterthought to success. It is not a consolation prize for the unsuccessful. Contentment is never in competition. It is simply about discovering our human potential to nourish others and make others feel like they are nourishment in every game we play.

Complacency	Contentment
I have sufficient	I have sufficient
I am satisfied with what I have	I can see other people's hunger
The other does not matter	I have surplus to repay debts
The world cannot be changed	I have resilience to reclaim patiently
	I have generosity to reinvest
	I can help the helpless feed others
	I can create ecosystems of responsibility
	I can create ecosystems of accountability
	I have faith and patience
	I cannot control the outcome

We are all born hungry. We all can feed and be fed. And we all have the option to die content.

Workbooks

The point of this book is to zoom out and look at yourself so that when you zoom back in, you are aware of your network, your relationship, your ecosystem and the world that will continue to be the same, but with new technology, even when you are gone.

Here are nine workbooks to help you on your contentment journey:
1. Self (who are you?).
2. Other (the ecosystem around you).
3. Fact, Fiction, Faith (how others see the world).
4. Expanding Mind (many truths)
5. Before Life, After Life (our inter-connectedness)
6. Transmission (beneficiaries and benefactors).
7. Object (your 'business' body that is driven by targets).
8. Process (your 'behaviour' body that does the task).
9. Subject (your 'belief' body that chooses trackers).

Escape the Bakasura Trap

1. Self

If you are a tree, what is your:	
Leaf (what do you crave)	
Root (who keeps you from being uprooted)	
Thorn (who protects you from hurt)	
Flowers and Fruits (what can you give in order to get something)	
Wood (what do people want to take that you do not wish to give)	
Imagination (what would you rather be)	
Ecosystem (who are the trees around you)	
Valuation (what you see as a valuable crop or useless/toxic weed)	

Workbooks

2. Other

- Any family member (not in your will)
- Any friend (no contracts between you)
- Employee (you approve their wages)
- Employer (they approve your wages)

If people around you are trees, do you see:				
Leaf (what they crave)				
Root (what keeps them from being uprooted)				
Thorn (what protects them from being hurt)				
Flowers and Fruits (what they let you have because they get something in exchange)				
Wood (what they resist giving but you want)				
Imagination (what would they rather be)				
Ecosystem (do they see you)				
Valuation (do you see them as valuable crop or useless/toxic weed)				

3. Fact, Fiction, Faith

Idea	Everyone's truth (fact)	Your neighbour's (belief)	Your truth (belief)	Nobody's truth (fantasy)
Newborn babies are helpless				
Humans are lonely				
Marriage is necessary				
God exists				
Rebirth is truth				
Justice exists in nature				
Equality exists in culture				
Pigs can fly				
Dragons exist				
Men are superior to women				
Disagreement is opposition				
Winning is success				
Rights exist in nature				
Nations are eternal				
Parents can exploit children				

Workbooks

4. Expanding Truths

Question	You	Your friend of opposite gender/sexuality	Your senior	Your junior
Have Capitalists and Socialists made humans less hungry or more hungry?				
Does technological change lead to psychological change? Has computers made us kinder?				
Are happy organised and clean societies open to immigration and tolerant of disobedience?				
Have you met revolutionaries who are homophobic?				
Does equality reduce diversity?				
Do victims want to solve the problem or punish the villain?				
Do rich societies slaughter more plants and animals than poor societies, per person?				
Do the poor want to be equal or do they want to be rich?				
Do the rich help as long as they stay rich?				
Does enforcement of tax and charity reveals human desire to hoard rather than distribute?				
Does desire for controlling the world and solving its problems is also cause of suffering (dukka)?				
Can material violence (ahimsa) cannot exist without material detachment (aparigraha)? Can mental violence (ahimsa) cannot exist without acceptance of diversity (anekanta) of human imagination?				

5. Before Life, Afterlife

	You	Your friend of opposite gender/sexuality	Your senior	Your junior
What do you use your phone to scroll more or to search more? What does it say about you?				
Have you consumed the past? Have you been affected by from your genes, your ancestry, you caste/community, their wealth, their legacy, their titles, their choices, their knowledge, customs and beliefs.				
Will the future consume you? Will the next generation be affected by your genes, your ancestry, your caste/community, your wealth, your legacy, your titles, your choices, your knowledge, customs and beliefs.				
Right now, who are you consuming? Which plants and animals are being slaughtered, which seas and skies and soils are being polluted, who are labouring to make your life possible?				
Right now, who is consuming you? Which plants and animals are your enterprises slaughtering, which seas and skies and soils are your investments polluting, who are you labouring for to provide for other people?				
Do you have surplus of wealth, power and knowledge? Are you in debt therefore? Who do you repay? Who do you plan to invest in?				

6. Transmission

Wealth, Power, Knowledge	What did you inherit	What were you taught	What did you earn and learn	What are you transmitting to insiders	What are you transmitting to outsiders
Property, Investments					
Debts					
Titles					
Relationships					
Science and Mathematics					
Politics and Economics					
History					
Literature and Art					
Faith and philosophy					
Rituals					
Critical Thinking					
Empathy					
Rights					
Responsibilities					
Trauma					
Hobbies					
Competition and Combat					
Collaboration					
Politeness					
Ambition					
Generosity					
Resilience					
Contentment					

Step 3 of 3: Feed More, to Sensitize Your 'Belief' Body

and fear. They did not see him as an endless source of knowledge to end hunger and fear itself.

As long as we fill our 'business' body with wealth and power and ignore knowledge, we will always be malnourished. We will remain Ravanas and Kuberas, who venerate Shiva's knowledge rather than striving to become one by becoming wiser.

Escape the Bakasura Trap

7. Object

What you have	Deficient (you are still seeking)	Sufficient (you do not seek more)	Surplus (you give to others)
Savings			
Investments			
Insurance			
Obligations			
Favours			
Pleasure			
Recognition			
Affection			
Friends			
Care-givers			
Knowledge			
Freedom			
Privilege			
Anxiety			

8. Process

Who does what	Your employer	Your employee	Your spouse	Your parent	Your child
Do you give them resources?					
Do they give you resources?					
Do you give them services?					
Do they give you services?					
Do you give them ideas?					
Do they give you ideas?					
Do you motivate them?					
Do they motivate you?					
Do you insult them?					
Do they insult you?					
Do you seek their company?					
Do they seek your company?					
Do you take initiative?					
Do they take initiative?					
Do you see them, or theirs?					
Do they see your, or yours?					
Do you see this relationship as an extraction, exchange, or trickery (performance shaped by evaluation)?					

9. Subject

Traits	Is that you?	Name a person you know who displays this trait.	Are they thinking about the self or the other?
Believes in the system			
Demands obedience			
Demands rights			
Does not want to interfere			
Wants to be seen as saviour			
Helps without expectation			
Does not bear grudges			
Does not think he matters			
Shows gratitude, not generosity			
Organizes events for others			
Outsources parenting to staff			
Enjoys gossip but not introspection			
Makes fun of other people's faith			
Performs rituals to please others			
More judgemental than curious			
More competitive than collaborative			

Workbooks

Traits *(conti.)*	Is that you?	Name a person you know who displays this trait.	Are they thinking about the self or the other?
Enjoys outsmarting people			
Needs to win an argument			
Enjoys letting others win in a game			
Sees oppression everywhere			
Sees good in villains, bad in victims			
Finds flaws on both sides of argument			
Sells an ideology constantly			
Writes off loans			
Includes everyone in the conversation			
Suspicious of all who ask for help			
Mocks nice people			
Repays debts			
Compliments people			
Shows rather than tells			
Lets people be themselves			
Spotlights the irresponsible			

Escape the Bakasura Trap

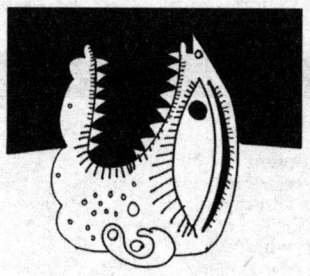

May contentment fuel your growth ...
and create delight wherever you go.

INDIA'S NO. 1 MYTHOLOGIST

DEVDUTT PATTANAIK

Shortlisted for the Atta Galatta Popular Choice Award 2022

HOPE

Wisdom to Survive in a Hopeless World